RESILIENT TRANSITION

SA'EED MUSTAFA

RESILIENT TRANSITION

COMBATING THE FEELINGS OF
STRESS & ANXIETY

Make Music, Meditation &
A Positive Mindset Your Healing Medicine

SA'EED MUSTAFA

Command Sergeant Major, US Army, Ret.

CONTENTS

Resilient Transition
Combating the Feelings of Stress and Anxiety
Make Music, Meditation, and a Positive Mindset
Your Healing Medicine
By CSM Sa'eed Mustafa, US Army Retired

First Edition

Cover design by Saheran Shoukat
Published in the United States by S4L Publishing

To my family, my team, my friends,
my fellow veterans, and my fans, thank you.

I truly appreciate your unconditional love, support, and
encouragement. It is because of you all that I have had a
Resilient Transition to civilian life, and thus I dedicate this
book to you.

INTRODUCTION

In the military, we learn to believe in a mission that is much bigger than ourselves—a principle demonstrated by countless women and men who've made the ultimate sacrifice for their fellow soldiers and country.

When we leave the military, many of us may feel a sense of loss, and the transition period to civilian life could be very disorienting to a service member who may feel they have lost their sense of purpose, identity, or mission in life. I initially felt this way, but thankfully I've found my purpose. I've made the transition. Now, my new mission is to help you do the same.

After thirty years of military service, I returned to my hometown in Highland Falls, New York, right outside the United States Military Academy at West Point. I witnessed some older military veterans, many of whom had been my elders when I was a young child, still passionately serving our community. One was

Command Sergeant Major Moses Carter, Sr., USA Retired, a pastor and one of my mentors. Others were World War II-era Buffalo Soldier, Sergeant Sanders H. Matthews, Sr., USA Retired; Sergeant First Class Sam Bass, USA Retired; Staff Sergeant Charlie Littlejohn, USMC Retired; and Sergeant Harold Brown, USA Retired. May they all rest in peace.

Following their lead, I began organizing talent events for the youth, holiday dinners for the homeless, and visiting the sick and shut-in senior residents. I became very close to local military WWII hero Sergeant Sanders H. Matthews, Sr., and learned more about his service as a Buffalo Soldier than I knew as a child. He had been stationed at West Point for most of his career and was a living legend. One day, I offered to take him to lunch in the Thayer Hotel at West Point. He declined, saying that he didn't feel comfortable to go because he still remembered not being allowed to go in there even as a soldier when the United States was still racially segregated. This motivated me to organize an event in 2015 to honor Sergeant Matthews in that same Thayer Hotel. That is when I met his lovely wife, Cora, who was ninety-eight years old at the time. When I ran for local office, she became my greatest mentor and political supporter until she passed away at 101 years old in 2020. These early experiences make me deeply grateful for the opportunity to return to my place of birth and serve the town that helped raise me.

Life, oh, what a journey!

Some people say that life's joy is in the journey, but often it can feel anything but that. Change can be difficult, for everybody. However, it can be especially hard for veterans due to the unique challenges resulting from their years of military service. Service members are totally immersed in military structure, culture, and values that may be different from regular civilian life. Some come into the service at a young age and end up devoting decades of their lives to it. Then one day, it's all over, and we are thrust into an unfamiliar situation trying to start a new life. Everything suddenly moves at a slower pace and we are surrounded by people who don't quite understand us. Transitioning may feel like starting over and it forces us to make uncomfortable adjustments. What am I supposed to do now? Should I work? Start at the bottom of the organizational ladder again? Doing what? Should I go back to school? Thinking about these questions, as well as the many options, is enough to induce significant stress and anxiety.

When I first came out of the military, I had a very hard time adjusting. The military had been my life since I was twenty years old and I never really thought about doing anything else. Like many service members, the military is in my DNA. I come from a long line of proud, patriotic military veterans, spanning back to World War I, at least. My maternal grandmother's brother, Sergeant Leon Tatum from Escatawpa, Mississippi, was a Buffalo Soldier assigned to the United States Military Academy to train the cadets in military tactics on horseback; he served for twenty-six years. He and his wife, my aunt Helen, are both buried at the West Point cemetery. My biological father, Dr. E.C. Foster was drafted in the late 1950s in Canton, Mississippi, and went on to work as a medic at Keller Army Hospital at West Point. My stepfather, George E. King, Sr., served during the Korean War era as an artilleryman, and later worked at the Montrose VA hospital as a civilian. Two of my younger brothers and I served in the same theater of operations during the Persian Gulf War in the early nineties; Patrick was later hit by an improvised explosive device during his second deployment to Operation Iraqi Freedom, ultimately losing his left foot in 2007. The love my family and I have for the military runs deep, and going through the transition from military to civilian life was one of the hardest things I've ever had to do.

Many of my other military brothers and sisters have also experienced challenging times during their transitions. I remember one of my former soldiers in the First Armored Division, one of the best I had served with in peacetime and war. She was a drill sergeant, had incredible courage, and was a fierce defender of her subordinates. Unfortunately, like many others who suffer from anxiety and a host of mental health issues, she fell from grace right as she got close to being eligible for retirement. Her unit leadership viewed her as a disciplinary problem, instead of someone who needed professional mental health care. This loyal and dedicated soldier was ultimately diagnosed with PTSD, as a result of experiencing constant enemy indirect fire attacks while in an isolated combat outpost in Iraq. The unit refused to accept the medical recommendations of the doctor treating her. Ultimately, they separated her from service rather than allow her to receive a pension, after she had put her life on the line multiple times for her country. The good news is, despite the lack of empathy from her military leaders, despite having suicidal ideations, and despite being homeless with two kids for a short time, her amazing resilience enabled her to bounce back and become victorious in the end. She is a post-traumatic stress survivor.

Her experiences and those of others I served with inspired me to write this book. My goal is to highlight the resilience within the veteran community and use these stories to help encourage as many veterans as I can to transition smoothly and easily into civilian life after their military career and to seek help in coping with mental health issues when needed.

I believe that when you know the hidden secrets of resilience, which I have discovered along my personal journey, it can make your transition as easy as brushing your teeth. I would love for life to be much easier for all transitioning service members than it was for me. Allow my experience and those of other veterans highlighted in this book to help you. I'm confident that it will help remove unnecessary pain, trials, and tribulations during your transition. If my methods are not helpful, please seek professional counseling or medical help, and please do not give up on yourself. The adjustment process for military men and women can feel so daunting that some become depressed, suicidal, or addicted to substances, which is not only sad but troublesome.

The reality is that any type of transition can potentially be a problem. Here are some recommended solutions, ideas, strategies, and concepts that could help you. Through the following sections and chapters, you will gain insight into navigating your life changes with minimal pressure.

Here's what you will learn:

We will kickstart this journey with some insights into how I transitioned from military to civilian life while offering scenarios we can all relate to. If you are a retired military leader struggling to adjust to your new environment, you may find these first chapters helpful.

You'll learn how to develop a resilient mindset and become a strong individual who is purpose driven, well adjusted and adaptable, able to problem-solve, and unafraid of challenges and change.

I will share with you something that I believe will

help you not only transition from the military to civilian life but also in **every** aspect of your life—health, wealth, and relationships. It is so profound and helpful that I would be remiss if I didn't share it with you.

What is it? The universal law of attraction.

I believe this metaphysical law is the most powerful law in the universe. Once you understand it, you can use it to manifest your goals and the new reality you desire. The law of attraction can change your entire trajectory, and with this book you'll realize how your possibilities are limitless.

You'll learn how to send out positive vibrations to get positive results and live in peaceful, stress-free optimism. And I'll teach you how to develop a proper mindset that will help you overcome and succeed.

We will explore the power of music on the brain and you'll learn techniques that will empower you to stay focused during the transition process. In addition, you will learn the importance of healing yourself with food, sleep, and exercise.

At the end of this book is a SPECIAL GIFT from me to you, which includes thirty days of positive affirmations, to go along with the practical concepts and materials I've included, all of which you can use right away.

I understand feeling stuck when everyone expects you to move on. Everyone would like a veteran to be a cheerful civilian, settle back into normality, quickly assimilate into society, get a job, get married, or do something with their lives to meet others' expectations.

However, this major life change is stressful and could bring a veteran to a very dark place. But you are not alone—I am right here with you as well as many others reading this book. Together, we will get the best of the transition phase, enjoy improved wellness from the inside out, and thrive wherever we are based.

I hope that you are as excited as I am to bring this information to you! It could literally change your life for the better from this moment forward. I want you to get excited about your new life as a civilian instead of floundering like a fish out of water. You can take all the skills you've accumulated in the military and apply them to your new life.

The question is, are you ready? Are you prepared to transition from where you are now to your new life?

If yes, then get your gear together, trooper, and let's do this together!

1
———

FIRST STEPS

Anyone who has experienced military life will likely tell you the same truth: Military life is often challenging, demanding, and periodically dangerous. It's an entirely different world from what most civilians have ever experienced, so returning to civilian life can be such a monumental process.

Many men and women who have served in the Armed Forces will admit that they've had difficulty adjusting as civilians, myself included. The adjustment complexities range from financial, emotional, cultural, psychological, and even physical; everyone is impacted in different ways.

Most veterans went into the military at a young age and developed their identity around military values, structures, and many things they became accustomed to in their military lives. For some of us, the positions and rank we acquire and the responsibility and comradery we develop bring us a sense of accomplishment and of self-worth. The pride we feel in serving our country and the bond we share with other patriots are unlike anything one could ever experience in other professions. So, there is a military institution and "culture" we get used to, and leaving that for regular life as a civilian could be disappointing, and for some veterans it could be downright scary.

Here is the first thing you should know if you are a transitioning veteran: It is normal to feel strange or a bit out of place when you return home. No, you are not weird. Neither are you overly dramatic or crazy. The beginning of the transition phase is almost the same unpleasant experience for all of us, but some are just better prepared and overcome it quickly. With time, it will get better.

My thirty years in the US Army came to an end when I had my retirement ceremony at West Point on October 8th in 2014. An amazingly prestigious event presided over by Colonel Landy Dunham and attended by Lieutenant General Robert Caslen closed my final door of military service. My mother, stepfather, wife, and three daughters, along with many family and friends from New York and Mississippi, were in attendance. It was almost like a movie as I reflected on my time in the Army.

After my retirement festivities were finally over, I found it extremely difficult to adjust back to civilian life because I had not ever seriously considered what I wanted to or could do after I got out. Additionally, I felt like I went back in time, and my perception was that everyone in my hometown saw me as the young person who had left there long ago versus the person I had become as a senior military leader with multiple combat deployments. There were times when it felt like it wouldn't get any better and I was just waiting until it was my time to die or until a better situation presented itself in another state or country. I certainly didn't want to die so soon, so although I was not suicidal, I started to realize how someone could fall into depression and despair as I slept for most of the day. I thought I would never fit into my new environment but I was totally wrong.

Initially I attempted to go to college in NYC and become a federal government employee, but after working in that environment for one year, I realized that was not what I wanted to do. I started to become active in volunteering, and it felt good to serve others in the community. Once I reflected on my military training, I remembered that we have been trained to adapt and overcome in any environment, and that is when things started to get better. I decided that if the Good Lord woke me up, I would get on with my day, deliberately stop being negative, and no more feeling sorry for myself or like I was out of place.

As I began to exude positive energy, I started to meet other veterans. By talking to them about how I felt, I shook the weight of imposter syndrome off my shoulder. I've found that it's important that veterans do not hold on to uneasy feelings but instead actively address them so that they wouldn't slip into states of depression.

I also used my passion for live music to feel better mentally. I began taking classes like Tai Chi at the VA hospital. I started practicing meditation and studying the universal law of attraction to be a more optimistic person. I started serving others without looking for any recognition or personal gain.

In 2014 I was asked to run for local elected office by a prominent Republican, but since I was not yet officially retired at that time and I was still trying to adjust, I declined. In the spring of the following year, I was invited to lunch by several members of the local Democratic party, who also asked me to run for office. I appreciated the fact that both groups thought enough of me to ask, but I really did not understand enough about local government to say yes to either and I had no party affiliation at that point. The second time I was asked, I agreed to solicit the opinions of my family and the elders in the community before I would make a decision. This time I felt mentally healthier after attending a couple of local board meetings, and I ultimately agreed to run for office and was blessed to become the first African American elected to be a councilman in my hometown. Then, I was nominated by New York State Senator James Skoufis and was honored with the New York State Veteran's Hall of Fame Award in 2020.

I share these achievements in hopes that they will

remind any veteran out there who is currently struggling, who may not have transitioned successfully, to never give up on themselves. Through my personal experience and extensive research, I know that anyone, but especially a military veteran, has the intestinal fortitude to have a resilient transition. This realization is the reason behind my motivation and passion in writing this book. I truly believe that it is absolutely necessary to offer solutions to you, other veterans and individuals who are in emotional pain.

Why is the Transition so Difficult?

Before analyzing the steps to ensuring a flawless transition, we should understand the "why." Generally, people understand that military-to-civilian transitions are taxing, but *why* is this often the case?

Why do veterans go through such challenging phases?

There are several reasons for a painful transition—some are general issues, and some are personal. We cannot highlight every personal issue at the root of each person's struggles, but we can analyze the common prevailing problems and offer solutions that could be applied to a soldier's specific situation.

Common Veteran Problems

One of the most discussed problems among veterans is related to none other than emotionally reconnecting with family and adjusting to a new role at home. We are frequently deployed around the world. We are often away for demanding training exercises, we have long absences due to military service, and we are forced to leave the family we love behind to figure out how to live without our presence.

On many occasions, when we come back, we must figure out where we fit in and how to reconnect with our family. They may have changed in many ways, or maybe we have. This reality requires that we consider the possible changes in their personalities, habits, and in many cases, their new desires. This is especially true with our children who change a lot as they grow up from children to teenagers and young adults. It can be painful when we leave our children behind, knowing that they will grow quickly, we will miss a lot, and they may be different from how we remember them; likewise, we may come back different from how they remember us.

It will take some families longer than others to reconnect once the veteran returns home. This is a normal part of the process, but it could have an adverse effect on the relationship between the veteran and the family members. The veteran needs to make a conscious and deliberate effort to reconnect with their spouse, siblings, kids, and even parents. This entails investing in and rebuilding relationships all over again. Patience is crucial during this process.

The Veteran Community Integration Problem

A significant challenge relates to the veteran not integrating into the community successfully. By *communities*, we mean groups of veterans where old and new members could meet and socialize.

Some existing communities can assimilate veterans on a general level (everyone comes in, attends the meetings, etc.). But some of these communities do not take the process down to the individual, so the veteran does not get the attention that they need and deserve. For some, attending such community events becomes a kind of obligatory routine without any meaningful impact or benefit.

Veterans in places with only a small veteran population face challenges with setting up new communities. We must admit that despite the progress we've made with raising awareness for the veteran community, new members require further assistance integrating.

The Workforce Challenge

The transition can also be extra tricky for veterans when they have the added pressure of preparing for a new career after military service. Many times, they begin preparing for positions they are not yet wholly ready to pursue.

I took a job with Homeland Security before I was even out of the uniform. While waiting three months for the background check to come back, I was required to send in a simple report once per week. Somehow I convinced myself that I could not fit within the organizational structure and ultimately left a well-paid, easy job only because I didn't have a positive mindset at that time.

Unfortunately, some veterans return home significantly traumatized by their military experience, and the necessity to work delays them from addressing their issues stemming from the trauma. In that state of trauma and with mental scars, they show up for work. This situation makes the transition process extremely hard. Lack of support from those around them only exacerbates the problem.

Loneliness

The transition process can be very lonely. When a veteran becomes a civilian, there could be feelings of isolation, as if nobody understands what you're going through. Everyone around you says, "I understand how you feel," but you wonder if they really do; how can they when they haven't experienced what you have? You feel lonely because your experiences as a military member differ so drastically from those of your family and friends. When you get party invitations, you're not eager to go and instead just wonder, "What am I going to do there? Who would I talk to?"

Loneliness can also stem from a longing for previous routines and predictable environment afforded by military life. In the military, we knew what to expect, and we were always prepared for emergencies. But as a civilian, initially you may not know what to expect. You may wake to wonder, "What's going to happen today?" The people around you already have their lives figured out, so they get on with their day as you stare out of the window. Succumbing to these feelings of emptiness is what sometimes drives veterans to depression and suicide.

Aside from depression, veterans also experience other psychological disorders such as post-traumatic stress disorder (PTSD), anxiety, and traumatic brain injuries (TBIs). Any of these coupled with substance abuse can become deadly.

Here's an overview of these disorders: PTSD[1] is a mental disorder that affects people exposed to traumatic events. They experience consistent and vivid flashbacks, nightmares, panic attacks, and severe anxiety in the aftermath of their trauma. These symptoms can continue long after the event has passed. Because of this illness, veterans can have negative thoughts about themselves and their transition to the civilian world. In most cases, they feel hopeless about the future, which makes them emotionally numb and unproductive. Because of the trauma, veterans can also feel guilt for surviving, especially if they have witnessed some of their comrades fall in battle. Some may feel that they deserved to die more than their friends. They think, "Why them and not me?" This could lead to trouble sleeping, depression, irritability, and self-destructive behaviors.

Depression, on the other hand, is more than a feeling of sadness or tearfulness. Depression[2] makes a person feel empty and hopeless. Because of this, they can have outbursts and feel frustrated even over minor issues. They can even lose interest in things they used to love, like sports or their hobbies. Often, people with depression feel heavy fatigue, which could lead to unproductivity and demotivation. There may also be an imbalance in how they eat and sleep; they either eat and sleep too much or too little, which could worsen their situation.

Next, anxiety. It is normal to experience anxiety when faced with change, but it's different when it turns into a disorder. When a veteran has an anxiety disorder, it could lead to an unsettling and dysfunctional life. Many people with anxiety disorders experience restlessness and panic attacks. They feel like they are always on edge. Because of this, they are irritable and worrisome wherever they go.

Substance abuse is another common psychological disorder experienced by veterans. Because they want to curb the pain and forget about their experiences, they drink in excess to numb the trauma—they self-medicate. But this behavior will only lead to further health issues and will only exacerbate their problems. There is a famous saying: "The same dose does not have the same effect." This is definitely true for alcohol. Once the body develops tolerance, the body will need more of it to feel its effects. In time, people will need more and more alcohol to get intoxicated. Some even opt for a more potent way to help them forget the pain, such as drugs. These destructive activities will be detrimental not only to your transition, but specifically to your potential new career and close relationships. Hence, there is a need to find healthier alternatives to push through the pain and heal from the trauma.

A number of UK studies[3] found, unsurprisingly, that mental health problems and military service are related, particularly for those deployed in combat areas. Researchers found that the most common psychological dysfunction is alcohol misuse, which is evident in most veterans, specifically those deployed to Iraq and Afghanistan. They also found that reservists were more likely to develop PTSD.

In further studies, researchers found that these mental health problems caused by traumatic experiences could worsen when service members get out of the military. Post-service factors play a significant role, including an unsuccessful transition to civilian life, loss of social support, marital problems, and many more.

Suicide remains a greater risk for younger veterans[4]

in both the US and the UK, and many former service personnel also experience social exclusion and homelessness. Without a healthy transition, the psychological distress experienced by veterans could worsen, leading to disorders, dysfunctions, and even suicide.

The service-connected trauma we get from being in the military often is debilitating. Unfortunately, in too many cases, family, friends, coworkers, and employers don't understand or lack the empathy to consider our pain. This is why veterans need to learn how to heal themselves from the invisible wounds, rise from the pain, and reestablish their positive connection to the world.

Adjusting to a Completely New Daily Routine

If you have ever changed jobs at any point in your life (even within the same sector), you would likely agree that the first few days will be challenging. You will feel like a fish out of water, surrounded by people you hardly know, trying to fit into the new work culture.

With veterans, we are not only talking about the change of jobs; we are talking about significant changes in almost every important aspect of life's circumstances. Yes, it is hard, but you can do it, and you will do it! Your daily routine is now completely different. Embrace the change. The process of adjusting to the smell of home-cooked pancakes in the mornings and not rushing out to do military drills will be one of pleasure if you recognize the value of being home with your family or at least out of harm's way. Waking up abruptly at night or having insomnia most nights was my reality in the first year of being back home. It was frustrating and made me irritable. There is just so much to adjust to, and it understandably takes its toll on veterans.

What is the Solution?

We know the problem, but what is the solution, and how can veterans ensure they have a smooth transition? It is important to note that the ideas you will find below are all practical steps, which means you have to be proactive but they are within reason.

For example, one of the steps urges the veteran to choose a civilian career that fits them. Now, after reading this, don't nod your head in agreement and go back to bed! You've got to decide on a career actively. Take inventory of your skills and experience, then think of what you would love to do even if you wouldn't get paid. All that is left is to write an effective resume and get ready to pour your heart and passion into this new endeavor.

I didn't get elected to public office by sitting at home and counting on my popularity; I had to actually get up, dress up, and go knock on thousands of doors and present myself to people. It was rather therapeutic to hear from the residents and take notes of what was important to each of them.

I know it's hard now, and I understand how difficult it can be in the beginning, but whatever you do, please don't ignore these steps or be dismissive about taking action. To experience real change, you must act. Understand that you can get a lot of help with what to do, and I will be right here cheering you every step of the way.

Get a Successful Veteran Mentor

I truly believe that the first step to having a smooth transition is to get help from a successful veteran mentor who represents who you want to be and where you want to go. Some veterans wallow in self-pity and so much pain because there is no one around them who has had the same experiences they've had.

However, with a mentor, you get an authentic connection with someone who offers a helping hand as you seek integration into civilian life. You may not have seen a mentor because you are not actively looking for one, but veteran mentoring programs are gaining popularity. If you haven't found one or haven't looked yet, please do. The key here is to have someone that has positive energy, who also brings value to your life in regard to the information and guidance that they provide. For me, one of my mentors is someone who I also mentor. Sergeant Major Keith L. Craig, US Army Retired, is a Hollywood executive and a published author. He provides me great mentorship on the entertainment business and was very instrumental in motivating me to complete my book. Keith is my classmate from the United States Army Sergeants Major Academy class 57, and his book is titled *Serving to Lead.*

Be Financially Prepared

Finances are one aspect some veterans don't regularly discuss. It may make them feel uncomfortable and even frightened of their new status. Well, you are now a civilian, and as a civilian you may need to make adjustments to your monthly personal budget. Making these calculations can keep you protected and help you remain cognizant of how much money you earn and spend.

Ignoring your financial realities puts an added and unnecessary strain on your life. You start to feel stressed when all financials accumulate; this is when the pressure hits. To be financially prepared, you've got to

- Start saving before leaving military life.
- Maximize all veteran's educational benefits, like the GI Bill.
- Save for your retirement.
- Protect your investments.
- Know your tax changes.
- Get life insurance.

Choose a Civilian Career

Leaving military life and transitioning as a civilian doesn't mean you go back home and lounge all day. This season is prime time in your life, and things will only become challenging when you don't keep yourself busy. You will have financial obligations (especially if you've got a family). Generally, working keeps you purposeful, which wards off depression and anxiety. Take your time choosing a career, and when you settle for one, remember to give it your absolute best, just like you did in the military.

Meet Other People in Your Desired Career

This step is so crucial because one of the reasons why veterans feel isolated and depressed is that they struggle to connect with regular civilians. But, my friend, you've got to try! You are in another world right now, one that thrives through social connection and not drills, missions, and machinery like in the military.

If you are to thrive in a new space, you've got to know how to interact, connect, and communicate with those in that new space. Since you might be starting a new career, get a head start by meeting people in that career field. Find out what you can expect, get tips, make the necessary connections, and make lasting relationships because you will need them as you evolve through civilian life.

Go Back to School

Before leaving military service, you should have already tried to figure out what you want to do with your life. Among the many options available to you, going back to school is one of them if that interests you. The military offers a tremendous educational benefit through the GI Bill and some colleges have special options for military members and veterans. You should take advantage of this if college is right for you. You will feel an initial hesitation, wondering if this is something you should do and overthinking how you will handle life in college. But listen, during a transition, the only way to move forward and make progress is to do just that. Always ensure that you are moving forward, and you won't feel the constraints of the transition.

Rely on Music

I began to listen to music frequently to deal with the frustrations of reintegration. Music elevates your mood, and whenever you feel distressed, you can turn to music to feel better. Music is also an emotional support system that takes you from the present reality into a positive state of mind.

Researchers have proven that music has many other psychological benefits aside from pleasure and contentment. It can help you manage pain[5], energize the body, and relax the mind. This is why psychologists use music therapy as an intervention to promote the emotional health of patients.

Neuroscientists[6] were able to study brain activity while the participants listened to music. Through MRIs and PET scans, doctors saw how multiple areas process sound. In their research, they found that music can help strengthen our bond with other people. In a study[7] conducted at Florida International University among young people, listening to music can improve confidence and character.

In addition, music also helps reduce stress, depression, and anxiety,[8] which are three of the common distresses felt by veterans. Music helps people cope with change and heal from trauma. It allows a person to challenge negative thoughts and focus on positive ones.

But, of course, the kind of music you listen to matters. Go enjoy your favorite music genres. But also remember to intentionally listen to conscious and helpful music—those that are happy, calming, and optimistic. One of my favorites is "Happy" by Pharrell Williams; give it a try to see how it elevates your positive vibrations.

How to Sustain an Empowered Transition

Now we know why veterans struggle with the transition process from military to civilian life. We also covered the steps you can take to ensure an easy transition, but what can we do to make sure we keep going forward?

Of course, no one wants to experience a sort of relapse into a negative mindset, but it happens when veterans fail to take steps to sustain a smooth transition. Sometimes the feelings of sadness creep up on us when we least expect it and—*boom!*—we are knee deep into the struggling phase again.

The following tips will help you sustain a healthy and resilient mental situation as you go through your transition.

Don't Isolate Yourself

Isolating while dealing with a challenging transition phase makes the entire situation worse. You may think that you need time alone. However, if you delay socializing with family and friends, they could have all moved away or even passed away by the time you are ready. Just remember that none of us are promised to see tomorrow, so live your life to the fullest starting today. In my case, instead of isolating myself, I took the opportunity to reconnect with my parents and appreciated the time I had to spend with them.

Avoid thinking that you need to stay away for a while. "I am fine by myself"—this idea is the root cause of anxiety and depression. The more you intentionally put yourself out there, the easier it becomes to adapt and effectively transition from military to civilian life successfully.

Get to Know Civilian People

Yes, I did mention earlier that you should join a veteran community to interact with other veterans. While that is great, you will also need to get to know other people without military experience. My initial attitude was civilians are so different that they are very strange people to me; now some of my best friends are people I have met after my retirement who have high regard for veterans but personally have never served.

There are so many people living in your community and many more on social media like my new friends. You should be open minded, curious, and approachable. Interact pleasantly as often as you can, and get to know civilian people; you will learn from them and expand your network.

Be Passionate, Whatever You Do

You've got to be passionate about whatever you do after coming out of the military. Initially, you may not exactly be doing what you wanted, but still give your best as you work on that task or job and keep working toward getting your dream job.

Passion keeps you focused and interested in what you do, especially at this stage when a lot of things don't seem to align. But if you remain passionate, you will find joy even in minor things.

First Steps | 39

If Needed, Seek Therapy

When needed, don't be afraid to get professional help. Not every veteran who separates or retires and goes back home needs therapy. For a more holistic process, you can try some natural alternatives; however, if you feel like you need a therapist, go to the VA hospital or other providers and book a session.

Therapy will help you maintain a healthy mental and psychological state. This is crucial because you need such balance to tackle the challenges that come your way. Don't be too shy or too proud to say, "I need help," and get it; you will be helping yourself a great deal. If I could do it, so can you.

Stay Fit and Active

Yes, you've got to stay fit and active to survive this stage. Some veterans experience a relapse because they don't keep their bodies busy after transitioning from military life. While in the military, we were accustomed to the drills and physical fitness regimen that kept us active. As a civilian, you may not get the same training, but you can still have a bit of it by being intentional with fitness. Exercise keeps you alert, strong (physically and mentally), and healthy. A healthy veteran is one with the potential to have a smooth transition. Ever heard of the saying "healthy body, healthy mind"?

Be Happy with Your Life

This step is crucial because, without it, you will probably remain a struggling veteran. You've got to try to be happy with your life and where you are at this moment for you to sustain all the efforts you've made. Be happy with the journey and be patient with yourself. Be happy with your results, and you will have something to look forward to daily. See the small steps you take as wins, and work hard not to be a grumpy, unhappy veteran—that won't help you. A negative attitude will be reflected in how you deal with civilians and apply to jobs, making it more difficult to transition.

The steps on how to ensure a smooth transition and sustainable ideas work together. For example, finding a mentor and seeking therapy are examples of getting third-party help. One will help you through the experiential aspects, and the other through the psychological aspects.

Your mentor understands what you've been through because they are also a veteran, so nothing you may say will be new information to them. Your therapist may not be a veteran, but they can help you through the psychological and mental issues such as depression, loneliness, and the struggle to adapt. You are bound to get better results if you use all steps together consistently.

This chapter is a foundational one that has laid the groundwork for all we will discuss in subsequent sections. Although we focused on the military to civilian transition using my experience as a case study, anyone going through a drastic change in life can relate to the ideas shared.

Again, to veterans who are struggling, I say to you: You are not alone, and I hope the details in this chapter will help you find direction and strength to transition with ease.

2

MY INTERNATIONAL WORLDVIEW

A while ago, I reminisced on some of my military experiences and the brothers and sisters I had met along the way. I started to wonder, "How is that soldier I met from Nigeria doing? How is the colonel from Germany doing? What about the lieutenant I met from Pakistan?" It made me curious about how they coped with their transition to civilian life and what are the problems they might have faced. I have served in so many countries and met many people along the way who have shaped my international worldview. So now we will focus on veterans from around the world, how their experiences and transitions are similar or different and why. Specifically, we will focus on the countries to which I was deployed and the home countries of the service members I have proudly served beside.

Everywhere around the globe, veterans, unfortunately, face very similar issues. Among the most common are homelessness, depression, substance abuse, mental illness, TBIs, and financial struggles. However, some countries have more support than others. Take the UK, for example. They have the National Health Service (NHS), which is available to permanent residents in the UK. It is essentially free healthcare funded through taxes, and private healthcare isn't necessary. The UK has around 2.4 million veterans and offers a priority[1] service for them for health issues related to their service. The NHS ensures that veterans are directed to the correct medical professional and in a timely fashion.

I asked a retired RAF commodore who had served for thirty-six years before culminating a successful career how he found his transition and if he ever had any struggles, mentally or physically. He responded that he had a fantastic transition without concerns or worries. He was actually ready to retire, in every sense. He has a good pension, a lovely house, a loving wife and children, and enjoys his days living by the sea, kayaking, and swimming. Someone like him in the Royal Air Force with the rank equivalent to a brigadier general does not represent the common soldier's experience; however, one can still replicate his mindset to gain similar results of a great quality of life post-military service.

Many veterans in the US often aren't so lucky, but some do have a good experience. There is no NHS and medical care like in the UK that covers everyone for free. American veterans can only get free healthcare for any illness or injury that is determined to be service connected. The American healthcare system is privatized, so if one has to go outside the VA system, it is expensive and leaves veterans exposed to great health risks. Suppose a veteran is homeless, severely depressed, struggling to secure a job, or struggling financially. How are they supposed to pay for the medical treatment they need?

In the US, we have the Department of Veterans Affairs, the VA.[2] It is a benefits system that traces its roots back to 1636, when the Pilgrims of Plymouth Colony were at war with the Pequot Indians. The Pilgrims ultimately passed a law stating that disabled soldiers would be supported by the colony. Then the Continental Congress of 1776 began to encourage enlistments during the Revolutionary War by providing pensions for soldiers who were disabled. In 1811, the first domiciliary and medical facility for veterans was authorized by the federal government. In the nineteenth century, the nation's veterans assistance program was expanded to include benefits and pensions not only for veterans but also their widows and dependents.

During the twenty years after World War II, services for veterans were expanded to include outpatient care, foster home care, trial visits, and increased work with the blind. There continues to be an ongoing debate on how to best deliver adequate healthcare to military veterans in the United States, particularly since the War on Terror has produced many post-9/11 veterans with significant medical and mental issues.

The VA has a sizable annual budget in place to care for veterans, which usually increases every year. Many veterans will benefit from this service. However, the waiting list for the help they need can be from three to twelve months due to the large veteran population. Many veterans cannot wait this long due to declining physical and mental health. This places our veterans at a higher risk for self-harm and suicide.

The US has around forty thousand homeless veterans.[3] Studies in the UK[4] estimate far fewer, with a study in 2008 estimating fewer than two thousand homeless vets.[5] These numbers speak for themselves.

I spoke to a US Army first lieutenant, and I asked him the same questions I asked the retired British RAF commodore. He told me that his transition into civilian life was very poor. He ended up getting divorced and drinking heavily for roughly seven years. He said the reasons for his struggle were not being a member of a team, loss of comradery, and not having a real mission. This highlights the importance of finding a new purpose after you become a civilian.

Responses from several other American soldiers varied, but many were similar in regard to the initial challenges with reintegration to civilian life. The hardest part of the transition was finding their place in their community and losing the comradery. Some went to college and found it challenging to connect with younger students due to their emotional maturity. Some went straight into work because they could not have supported their family if they didn't. In some cases, marriages broke down due to PTSD and alcohol addiction.

A US Navy sailor who served for five years informed me that he had his whole transition planned out on paper. It sounded effortless whenever he read it to himself. However, once reality set in, there was nothing easy about it at all. He came out just as the COVID-19 pandemic hit. Due to how the pandemic affected the job market, he found it extremely difficult to secure employment. Eventually, he found a job working at a local supermarket, which was not what he wanted for his life, but he had bills to pay. When working at the supermarket, he discovered he had PTSD after the fire alarm unexpectedly went off. His reaction led him to seek counseling. He said, "The hardest thing to deal with was no longer being a part of something big anymore.... Maybe things have changed since I got out, but in my experience, while you are in the military, it consumes your entire life. When you adapt to that life-style it is very difficult to reverse. No matter how committed you are while in uniform, once you leave, nobody cares."

I then had the pleasure to talk with a US Air Force sergeant who served for ten years. He told me that his transition went perfectly. He began mapping his methodology for change a year before retirement while completing a degree during his service. However, he has struggled with mental health and anxiety issues every day since retiring. Although he feels fortunate to have his children, a lovely home, a good job, suicidal thoughts continue to arise. He refuses to give in to these thoughts and has taken up a new hobby: woodworking. "Seven years ago, I couldn't make a thing. Now I can hand-cut dovetails like a pro and pretty much look at a piece of furniture and build it. It is what I do when I am stressed and need to relax and think," he shared with me.

Our neighbors in Canada have very similar benefits and organizations to the US. They have the Veterans Affairs Canada,[6] which supports disability compensation, rehabilitation, income support, health services coverage, and career transition support. Regardless of the positive aspects of their healthcare system, after speaking to a Canadian veteran, it is clear that they also share the same difficulties with transitioning to civilian life, in particular, access to prompt healthcare and lead time between receiving pension and veteran benefits.

Now let's go to India. I spoke to a former colonel and deputy commander who served in the Indian Army. He told me that military life and civilian life in India could not be more different. Life in service offers many comforts and privileges. If you are fortunate enough to retire at a higher rank, there is a good chance you have savings and can live reasonably well after retirement. He told me that higher-ranking service members are highly respected among society and seen as being better educated and more vibrant than an everyday citizen. However, he informed me that while veterans may appear this way, this is not the case behind closed doors. Many veterans in India turn to alcohol as a coping mechanism.

In 2012, shortly after returning from my second deployment to Iraq as the battalion command sergeant major (CSM) of the 123rd Brigade Support Battalion, I was selected to be stationed in Germany for the first time in my career, and assigned as the garrison CSM in Wiesbaden. In that role, I had the honor of working with many great civilians both American and German, and I also frequently interacted with members of the German Army and political figures. It was a very prestigious job and I was really good at it; all the while I was masking my stress, anxiety, and depression issues. Looking back from a wellness perspective, I now can see how the lack of self-care for many years and improper work-life balance eventually caused me some mental health issues. It was my German military friends who said to me, "You Americans live to work, and we German's work to live."

One of the most positive things from that period of my life was being the founder and president of the Wiesbaden Sergeants Major Association. Through that organization, I received some amazing mentorship about transitioning to civilian life from retired sergeants major, among whom was a graduate of the fifth class of the United States Army Sergeants Major Academy.

A few of our German partners from the German Army and the German American Friendship Club were also members of our association, and I learned that a German soldier's pay is relatively good, with one of the biggest "danger pays" compared to other countries. If a soldier is harmed either mentally or physically and it reduces their ability to work by 30%, they are guaranteed work by the Bundeswehr—Germany's unified armed forces—until they retire. The Bundeswehr offers several vocational training programs that service members can complete alongside their military duties. These programs qualify soldiers for jobs after serving. Many of them become successful in carpentry, engineering, mechanics, and many more. Service members are also offered a one-off "transition easing" payment in their last paycheck. We know financial problems are prevalent among veterans, and this financial aid is helpful.

But what about German service members who may have PTSD or a TBI struggling with the transition mentally? From my conversations and research, it seems that there is a constant battle for the German military to recognize these disorders. A soldier I know had traumatically witnessed his fellow soldier die in a suicide bombing. He'd been unable to obtain critical medical care and trauma and became an alcoholic and eventually homeless. He fought for help for years and was only recently granted ex-military housing through relationships with other veterans. Luckily, his nightmarish flashbacks are now under control.

I also wanted to look at Korea, as I served in South Korea three times during my career. Since 1957, Korean men must serve in the military for a minimum of two years of a mandatory commitment. Alternatively, they can serve the US army stationed in South Korea; soldiers in the US Army are called KATUSA, or Korean Augmentation to the United States Army. Often, when service is mandatory, the feelings toward it are negative. In most other countries, men and women choose to join the military. They willingly do the mental and physical training—it is an experience they want. An article[7] from 2012 shares the experience of a soldier who was forced to enlist. Reflecting on his experience, he says that he feels he can achieve anything with the mindset he developed from serving.

Lastly, let's look at Pakistan. I spoke to a still-serving officer, who informed me that the average retirement age for soldiers is forty years old. The main struggle with going back to civilian life is financial difficulty. The salary and pension of service members in Pakistan are relatively not great, which means it is hard to have savings. Once they retire from military service, they still need to work to pay their bills and look after their families but often lack the skills and education required for a well-paid job.

A common problem for veterans from every corner

of the world is the lack of benefits and how long it takes to receive them, such as VA benefits. It can be a long-waiting, tiresome process that should be made easier and more accessible for our brothers and sisters who serve their country. Struggles such as these are among the reasons many veterans feel uncared for once they leave the service.

Veterans across the globe appear to face some of the same issues. Local governments and charities provide support where possible, all with different accessibility and quality levels. Each system has its successes and flaws, but much more support is still needed. They need access to prevention, diagnostics, treatment, rehabilitation, education, counseling, and community support. Veteran-centered medical and health services need to be widely available to all who have served, especially to those who served in combat.

Some veterans may not know the resources available or how to apply for the help they need. They may fear that asking for help could affect their current job. They may worry they will face discrimination because of the stigma surrounding mental health, or they may have transport or other accessibility issues. There are so many possible barriers between veterans getting the help they need and deserve, but this must change.

3

SUICIDE PREVENTION

The connection between veterans and suicide is, quite frankly, profound. In 2019, according to the VA, the suicide rate for veterans was 1.5 times higher than non-veterans. In the United States, it is estimated that twenty veterans commit suicide every single day.

Suicide is the second-highest cause of death in the US military. There is a link between suicides and veterans struggling with financial and career difficulties. There are over forty thousand homeless veterans who may also suffer from mental and physical health issues. Statistics[1] show that veterans suffering from a mental illness or addiction are more likely to commit suicide, with one in ten veterans diagnosed with a substance disorder.

One of the leading causes of mental disorders among veterans is TBIs. When head injuries happen, they often don't get timely care that is critical for recovery out of worry of being non-deployable, thus causing difficulties in obtaining appropriate treatment once the veteran is in civilian life. Studies[2] in 2018 showed that veterans who had suffered from more than one TBI were twice as likely to have suicidal intentions than those who had not. This is because TBIs are linked to addiction, insomnia, depression, anxiety, headaches, memory problems, and irritability.

Until now I still frequently experience insomnia and have been dealing with it for some time. From what I can remember, it started during my 2009-2010 deployment with the 121st BSB 4th Brigade Combat Team to Tallil, Iraq. Insomnia can be short-lived or prevail for years and years. I could easily succumb to insomnia and spend my days catching up on sleep. It could have me not applying myself to my work and giving up on my goals and ambitions. But I refuse to let this happen through my mindset, my high vibrations, and my sanctuary in music! If I can do this, you can too! And as you read through this book, I will support you every step of the way.

In 2016, the Office of Suicide Prevention reported[3] that veterans accounted for 18% of the US suicide population, which has sadly increased every year. These figures are genuinely heartbreaking. Some of our brothers and sisters we proudly served with struggled with an illness and could not see the light at the end of the tunnel. This is one of the many reasons I am so passionate about helping with the transition to civilian life. These statistics must improve, and support must be made more accessible and freely sought.

I am now going to share with you a personal experience, a loss, that many of us veterans know too well.

This book is dedicated to my battle buddy, my 1988 Camp Carroll Korea championship basketball teammate, my close friend, my brother from another mother. Orlando was about six feet, two inches tall and about two hundred pounds of muscle. Very personable and had the gift for gab. He was a good-looking guy with a strong leadership presence and was extremely athletic. The ladies loved him, and although he could be imposing of a figure, he was a mama's boy at heart. Orlando's dedication to the military and commitment to duty were unmatched!

We met in 1988 in Petersburg, Virginia, at Fort Lee, where we took classes to change our military occupational specialty to Quartermaster Warriors. We instantly became friends during physical training after getting smoked by the drill sergeants of Fox Company. A few months passed, we both graduated and then went our separate ways, only to meet again later that year in Korea, where we were both stationed. We were shocked and happy to see each other again. We became inseparable for the next year, playing sports together, coaching a women's basketball team together, even getting our clothes tailored at Mr. Kim's shop together!

The year went by fast, I went from Korea to Georgia, then later to the Gulf War in Iraq and then back to

Korea after the war was over. Orlando went to Fort Polk, Louisiana, and then eventually became an Army recruiter. We were on separate journeys, but we always found a way to stay in touch in the early years of our friendship. But eventually life got in the way and we weren't able to keep in touch as much as we would have liked.

In 2003, I was back in Virginia, and there he was in the flesh! We were reunited. My dear friend was now a master sergeant and had recently completed his time as the first sergeant of Uniform Company, 262nd Quartermaster. I was an incoming first sergeant, scheduled to take over the same organization. It was so great to see him again and catch up.

More years went by, and after twenty-six years of service, Orlando retired. We still kept in touch but not nearly as often. In 2009, I was deployed to Tallil Air Base, Iraq. Before I departed, I returned to my home in Fort Bliss, Texas, for two weeks of leave and bumped into a mutual friend. He asked me if I'd heard the news about our friend Orlando. I was taken aback. "No, but I have been meaning to call him," I said. "He has been on my mind. What's going on with him?" I will never forget what he said to me next—I can still hear the words echoing.

"He blew his brains out."

I was in shock. *Why? When? How? Why didn't I call him? Why didn't he call me? No, not my brother—he was so strong, so full of life—he couldn't be gone.*

For many veterans, as soon as they retire, they feel alone, like no one cares. No one checks in on them. They feel lost without the comradery of their military unit. Was this how Orlando felt? For a long time, I carried a sense of guilt and a heavy heart. It wasn't until I read a beautiful poem written by another good friend as a tribute to our fallen veterans that I found peace with the loss of my brother. The poem immediately made me think of Orlando. I realized I should remember him as I knew him and celebrate his life. I am thankful to the poem's author, retired US Army Quartermaster Regimental Command Sergeant Major Jose Silva, for allowing me to honor Orlando by placing his amazing poem in this book.

I hope Orlando's story highlights how serious suicide among veterans is. Veterans must support each other, stay in touch, pick up the phone or send an email or text, and be present for their brothers and sisters. One phone call could have the biggest impact. That one call could be the one they desperately need.

To help veterans come together and support each other, I have created an annual suicide awareness and prevention gala in New York. The gala has been running for five years now, and veterans from all over the US attend. It is a night of comradery, food, music, reminiscing, and support, where veterans can once again feel like a member of a unit. They can be mentored, find their purpose, and become valuable members of my veteran movement to care for each other and always feel connected. My goal is to create a powerful network that leaves no veterans behind. They no longer will feel alone, and we will help mentor and coach them in their transition into civilian life. Our new morning physical training will be yoga and meditation sessions and our weekly sergeants time training will be to teach them about positive vibrations and the laws of attraction in hopes that one day, no veteran will follow the path that my best friend Orlando sadly did.

Rest in peace, Master Sergeant Orlando Cortez Simmons. Until we meet again, my friend.

Remember Me

*Remember the warriors of the past
for I have found my place among them.*

*Sorrow has brought us together
as in the day when the shophar announced
that I had fallen asleep
while embracing my wings
and risen beyond the clouds.*

*But let your heart not be troubled nor broken
for above the stars of the midnight sky
my gaze will always be upon you
from a place where eagles dare not fly.*

*So don't let my absence sadden your spirit
nor allow the sorrow to burden your soul.*

*Remember the years you were with me
and those special moments
we valued as gold.*

*Remember me when you stare in the mirror
when you hold a grainy photo
perhaps hidden in your bag.*

*Remember me when you read a faded letter
from a ship in the Pacific
the mountains of Korea
or the jungles of Vietnam.*

Think of me

*and when you think of me and ponder
always do so with a smile
and be happy, for in Earth's glory
nothing is perennial
good or bad.*

*Yet if I'm forgotten in some moments
and later remembered, do not grieve.*

*Contemplate my folded flag,
lift your thoughts beyond those stars*

and let me whisper in your ear.

Remember the warriors of the past
for I have found my place among them.

—CSM José Luis Silva-Díaz, USA Retired

2021

4

LEARNING RESILIENCE FROM CELEBRITIES

Military life and celebrity life are similar in that routine, working out, and purpose are integral in both. Rather abruptly, as soon as you retire or separate from service, there is an immediate void in your life that could be hard to fill. Service members and celebrities both operate under high stress levels. Similar to celebrities, who constantly face external pressures, soldiers are also held to a higher standard than regular citizens. Both groups sacrifice their private lives and are held to a certain behavioral code. These requirements contribute to their stress.

So many incredibly talented and famous people have dared to share their stories about battling mental illnesses. Big homes, bigger bank accounts, fancy cars, and hordes of fans—it could seem like celebrities have it all. But fame doesn't protect you from mental health problems.

Every person has their own hidden struggle, and what seems perfect could have a lot of distress behind closed doors. This is true for celebrities[1] as well. As we become more aware of how mental health issues affect our everyday lives, it becomes increasingly important to talk about our personal experiences and to know it's okay to seek help. Celebrities who use their platform to talk about their depression and other mental health issues are normalizing having issues as well as getting help to take care of our mental health. In working with people with mental health challenges, I've found that dialogue offers a therapeutic opportunity to share stories and remind us that we are not alone in our struggles.

I, retired Sergeant Major Sa'eed Mustafa, will no longer be afraid to say publicly that I have my own ongoing struggles with service-connected transition anxiety, sleep disturbance, insomnia, nightmares, PTSD, and depression. I had my first visit with a professional therapist at the end of my active-duty career. Directly after my retirement and upon returning home, I began seeing a therapist at the VA hospital. I'm happy to report that, as a PTSD survivor, I'm now consciously using the solutions I've learned, which I'm sharing in this book, to control and manage my mental health wellness. If you are suffering from these types of issues, just know that you are not alone, and we can live a happy and healthy life—one of service to others in our community.

I remember visiting a friend who's a nurse at the Veterans Administration Hospital. She told me that she was quite surprised with the younger veterans as they were stubborn and did not readily listen to the staff. So, one day I had an appointment at the VA. I wore my military hat, which at the time I did not wear very often. It said "CSM Retired," showing my rank. I was walking down the hall when I crossed paths with two young gentlemen. As soon as they saw my hat, they started assuming the Parade Rest position, which symbolizes respect and discipline within the military community. They clasped their hands behind their back and greeted me.

"Good afternoon, Sergeant Major," they said.

I felt like I was back in the Army, and I told them, "I'm proud of you guys. Both of you are here to get help, and you are in the right place. You shouldn't feel that you are any different from others because we all have our struggles." I gave them my business card and asked them to call me if they needed to talk. We then said our goodbyes and walked off.

My friend, the nurse at the hospital, saw all of this and asked me how I pulled this off. They were the guys she had previously told me about. They didn't have respect for anyone. They didn't listen to anyone, so it surprised her that they humbled themselves for me. I think it was because we military people understand and recognize each other. They knew that in the military world, I was a person that had something to offer them, perhaps some knowledge or experience. Those young men demonstrated that there is still some level of military culture, discipline, and respect deep down inside most of us who are now called veterans.

So on that day I decided to embrace the fact that the Army had invested a lot of money and time to train me to be a leader and that I have something to offer the veteran community. And as such, I am saying that it is okay to get help and take care of your mental health. I did it. And so have many other people. I've had my struggles, and I intend to be more vocal about it now.

When I was in the Army, having mental health struggles was looked upon as a weakness. Now I want soldiers, veterans, and others to be comfortable with telling their truth and to feel free to talk about their feelings and experiences. I'm so glad to see society start to normalize this, and many of my celebrity friends are leading the charge. My hope is that this movement will motivate the younger soldiers to seek help.

If I can open up to tell my story, you can too!

Some of the most influential voices out there belong to celebrities. People look up to them so much; sometimes they would follow anything that celebrities said or did. In recent years, we've witnessed many celebrities speaking about their experiences with mental health issues. I've seen the positive effects that these celebrities can have, particularly on the younger generation, and the overall impact celebrity voices can have on a person's ability to speak about their own experiences.

Professional Athletes

Athletes, be it individuals or members of a team, face enormous pressure to perform well and win. A lot of people are counting on them—their fans, the sponsors, their handlers, the team's owner, and many others—especially when there is big money involved. The physical and mental demands of the sport can sometimes be overwhelming.

Naomi Osaka,[2] a Japanese tennis player and the current world number 2, having won four Grand Slam championships, has been vocal about her struggles with depression since 2018. Other athletes[3] who have done the same include Zack Greinke, Serena Williams, Ronda Rousey, Ricky Williams, and Picabo Street.

Such disclosures from celebrities regarding their mental health struggles enriches the discussion of what it means to have mental illness. The public learns that it is okay to have a mental health diagnosis and seek treatment, thus lessening the stigma.

Professional Athletes after Retirement

Just like retired veterans, professional athletes have an increased risk of having mental health issues, including anxiety, depression, and substance abuse, during their career and following their retirement. Like soldiers, athletes train with a set routine, big purpose, rigorous workout, and the goal to be the best. When they are not physically training, they are mentally training. They would see specialists such as physical therapists and sports psychologists to make sure they are in the best physical and mental shape they can be to compete. Once they stop training so vigorously, days may feel empty. Even if it is 100% their choice to retire and think it is the right time, they still may feel this emptiness. It is the same with soldiers. When you had something to train for, it gave you purpose. Now you no longer have a goal, and you are not sure how to spend your days. A lack of purpose can leave you feeling worthless or hopeless.

Most athletes reach their peak at a young age and retire from their competitive sport early in life. Nowadays, athletes have many opportunities to get a degree while pursuing their professional sports, opening career options for them when they retire. Most professional athletes are used to earning a significant income and are provided free perks throughout their careers. They are used to getting attention and being recognized by the public. Once they retire, the recognition may disappear. They may find it difficult to sustain the lifestyle they are used to. It may feel devastating for them to see their social media following decrease over time. These factors can contribute to a retired athlete feeling unfulfilled and may lead to depression and anxiety. They may turn to substance use to help mask these feelings.

They may have a new career lined up, but they most

likely won't need to spend as much time and focus on training. If they were previously training for the Olympics or a national championship, transitioning to a desk job may not seem motivating and exciting. Many retired professional athletes end up coaching others in their sport. This can be a very fulfilling career, and a lot of retired athletes enjoy it. But it takes time to make the transition.

So, like them, don't be hard on yourself if you are feeling down and disappointed with your transition. Allow yourself to feel the feelings you are experiencing now, then refocus on new hobbies, activities, and a job you enjoy.

Actors and Actresses

When they are at the peak of their careers, actors are constantly scrutinized. It would seem that some people are just waiting for them to fail or make a mistake. Their personal life is no longer private as fans and the media always crave information about their lives: who they are hanging out with, what designer brand they are wearing, what they are eating, and so on. Eventually, this becomes annoying, then frustrating, and ultimately affects their mental health. There are now hundreds of famous actors and actresses[4] and other celebrities who have admitted to having depression and other mental health struggles.

Goldie Hawn[5] spoke about struggling with depression in her early twenties. She explains how stardom and fame at an early age were tough to process for her. It was something she never craved for. There were instances she couldn't even go outside in public. Her personal life was invaded, and she had to go to a psychologist to work through that phase of her life.

Oprah[6] is another Hollywood celebrity who has been one of the most prominent voices in the conversation about mental health. By speaking of her personal experience, Oprah has inspired thousands of people to come forward with their mental health struggles, leading them to resources that offered a greater sense of acceptance and personal joy.

Another renowned Hollywood name who has admitted to having struggles with depression is Dwayne "The Rock" Johnson.[7] He did an interview with *Express* and told readers, "You're not alone." He has also tweeted to his millions of followers, raising awareness about mental health across race and gender.

Many celebrities are making it their mission to normalize conversations around mental health issues, bring awareness, and encourage others to get help.

Musicians

Just like athletes and actors, musicians have also shown remarkable resilience to mental illness. One study[8] found that more than 73% of musicians report having faced a mental health disorder like depression. Famous musicians[9] like Ray Charles, Leonard Cohen,[10] Brian Wilson, John Denver,[11] Bruce Springsteen,[12] and Eric Clapton have shared their experiences with depression and other mental illnesses and have shown the world that it's okay to talk about it and even more so to seek help. Their music increases awareness of mental health and normalizes psychiatric illnesses. Our musical icons, although seemingly larger than life, are actually just like us, struggling with similar issues and overcoming mental illness.

Many musicians also suffer from substance abuse, which contributes to their mental illness or they may be self-medicating because of it. Whichever the case, I would like to echo what others have said that substance abuse is never an effective nor productive means to cope with mental illness.

Celebrities Serving to Counter Mental Health Problems

In 2017 I booked three-time Grammy Award nominee and Tony Award winner Melba Moore for the second annual Town of Highlands Juneteenth celebrations in Highland Falls, New York. The following year, we did some work together for my annual Veteran's Resiliency Gala at Bear Mountain Inn. Spending time with Melba during rehearsals and after her performances allowed me to witness a celebrity who has come back from adversity and hardship. She is the epitome of a resilient transition. Her faith in God and her routine of eating healthy, drinking lots of water, being kind, and focusing on her craft was a living example of what right looked like and was very helpful to me.

I enjoyed meeting and hanging out for a day with American stand-up comedian, actor, and film producer Mike Epps, best known for playing Day Day Jones in *Next Friday* and its sequel *Friday After Next*. Mike is extremely funny in real life as he is in character. He is highly intelligent and, more importantly, he is also very resilient.

I also got a chance to spend significant time with some celebrities who came to entertain and raise the morale of the cadets at West Point during the pandemic. The list includes three-time Grammy Award winner Wyclef Jean, who dealt with significant controversy when he attempted to run for President of Haiti. I bought Wyclef an entire military combat uniform, which he performed in for the cadets for two hours straight at Eisenhower Hall theater on March 6, 2021. His energy, humility, and intelligence were three traits that positively impacted me.

Four-time Grammy Award nominee Flo Rida has sold over 100 million records. He also came to West Point to raise cadet morale during the academy's Wellness Week. He recognized that they experience a lot of pressure during their time at the nation's premiere military university. When speaking with Flo, I realized that the common thread between all those phenomenal and famous celebrities that I had the pleasure to observe includes their faith, love for their craft, and their humility.

In many ways I was like them in the military world when I served in the United States Army and reached the rank of command sergeant major. I've had conversations with all of my celebrity friends about follow-up projects we will be doing on other military installations in the future. Flo Rida showed great interest in helping me address the mental health and well-being of active military members and veterans through wellness concerts for the troops around the world.

Although I did not meet him when he came to West Point, I also want to give a shout-out to Emmy- and Golden Globe-winning actor Gary Sinise,[13] who has been standing with the men and women of the United States military for almost four decades. His support of Vietnam veterans started in the early eighties, and in the nineties he began working with the Disabled American Veterans organization. He and the Lt. Dan Band, named after the double-amputee veteran he played in the groundbreaking movie *Forrest Gump*, have been performing worldwide since early 2004 on military bases, for charities, and at fundraisers in support of our troops, veterans, and their families. The Gary Sinise Foundation is now in its tenth year in its mission to support not only the military and vets but also first responders and others in need through entertaining, educational, and inspirational community-building programs. In 2020, he was awarded the Patriot Award[14] by the Congressional Medal of Honor's Society for his decades-long service and dedication to military and veteran communities.

Demi Lovato and Rihanna are part of a younger generation of musicians that are not only increasing public awareness of mental illness but also doing good work through their own foundations or partnering with organizations. During the COVID pandemic, Demi Lovato launched The Mental Health Fund,[15] which was able to raise about $2 million within a few months for crisis counseling, and Rhianna's Clara Lionel Foundation[16] donated $15 million for mental health services.

Taraji P. Henson,[7] a Golden Globe-winning actress, has been a tireless advocate for addressing mental health and mental health disparities in the Black community, and never have such efforts been so necessary. According to the National Alliance on Mental Illness,[17] more than 17% of non-Hispanic Black adults in the United States struggle with mental illness, including depression and anxiety. She founded the Boris Lawrence Henson_Foundation[18] in 2018, whose vision is to "eradicate the stigma around mental health issues in the African-American community." It is named after her father, a Vietnam War veteran who struggled with post-traumatic stress disorder. She herself has admitted to having depression and anxiety.

My goal is to collaborate with celebrities who have demonstrated resilience and or have spoken about mental health issues. Their courage and example have helped me in my own transition. I have observed them closely, and they have inspired many, including me, a combat veteran.

I believe that social media can also serve as a compelling means to raise awareness of mental health and to normalize talking about it. We can start by using the hashtag #ResilientTransition. Testimonials and continued effective health communication can and will make a difference.

If you are struggling with mental health issues, please get help today so you can overcome and cope with your diagnoses and learn to channel your energy into something you can be proud of one day.

You can overcome depression. It doesn't have to rule your life or hinder you from accomplishing great things or achieving your dreams.

In the next chapter, I am going to talk about how you can develop a resilient mindset so you can find the strength to stay true to yourself and overcome your struggles.

Celebrity Veterans Who Have Transitioned into Civilian Life

Below are some celebrities who served their country before they became famous!

- Morgan Freeman — US Air Force, 1955-1959
- Tom Selleck — California Army National Guard, 1967-1973
- Clint Eastwood — US Army, Korean War, 1953
- Chuck Norris — US Air Force, 1958-1962
- Gene Hackman — US Marine Corps, 1946-1951
- James Earl Jones — US Army, Korean War, 1953
- Gal Gadot — Israel Defense Forces, 2005-2007
- Jennifer Marshall — US Navy, 1999-2004
- Robin Quivers — US Air Force, 1975-1978
- Jimi Hendrix — US Army, 1961-1962
- Elvis Presley — US Army, 1958-1960
- Adam Driver — US Marine Corps, 2002-2004

5

DEVELOP A RESILIENT MINDSET

A resilient transition involves moving from one phase of your life to another despite challenges and winning in life. But we cannot experience this if we don't foster a resilient mindset because our mindset controls our outcomes. You are not different from the content of your mind.

Some people have ascribed resilience to survival. They think it is tied with surviving a particular phase of life and then moving on to survive the next stage. Yet, strength goes beyond the concept of survival; in fact, it is not about surviving anything.

Resilience is more about an individual's ability to take on a difficult task and still maintain balance. Resilience signifies that even if you lose your balance, you could bounce back and keep on moving. Resilience cuts across all aspects of your life: physical, emotional, spiritual, and mental. It is the flexibility you develop that equips you for change even in the face of misfortune.

Survival is only about the physical. It is a mindset that makes you think only about the present moment without preparing for the future. So, with survival, you are just contemplating today and what you can do today; you are not thinking beyond this day. If you only focus on today, how do you intend to transition and make plans for your life?

If you have been in survival mode or had a survival mentality, it is time to make changes by building a more resilient mindset. That is how you can experience resilient transitions. You can train yourself to become resilient by being intentional with your thoughts and ensuring that you have an overcomer's approach to life.

That training starts with your mind and contemplations since you cannot give what you don't have. You cannot become resilient when you don't even have resilient ideas. Considering that your thoughts drive your action, the mind is an excellent place to start.

First visualize what you want, then move toward it. See it happening, and it will happen. Start building resilience in your thoughts because that is the core aspect of your life experiences. Since this is training, there will be days when you feel more resilient and days when feel like you are not making progress. Instead of giving up, you need to push yourself on such difficult days, for that is how you build a resilient mindset.

Have you ever prepared for a marathon? If so, you may agree that it tends to be a very taxing process that requires intense training and workout to build your muscles. The stronger your muscles, the more stamina and endurance you build for the race. While training, you may feel energetic and strengthened on certain days and under the weather on other days.

If you are ardent about triumphing in a marathon, you need to show up on both kinds of days and proceed with your training until race day. This illustration with a marathon is quite fitting as it encourages you to understand some truths about building a resilient mindset:

- First, you wouldn't always "feel" resilient, but you need to transcend feelings and do what is expected and required.
- Second, you need to continue training even when you are dealing with very harsh conditions. The athlete who wants to win the race trains under the sun and the rain; the person who wants to become resilient must push their boundaries regardless of what life throws at them.
- Third, you've got to practice and practice until resilience becomes a part of your life, thoughts, and mental process. You should get to the level where even in the face of life's

storms, you have only one option: to keep propelling forward.

When you think about a resilient mindset, think about a moving train that doesn't stop until it reaches its destination. If you are a moving train, life would have no other choice but to pave the way for you as you transition because you have empowered your mind to become resilient.

The transition phase will test you; it would strain you because you would be changing the structure in your life, but guess what—those trying times are the BEST times to build resilience. If you don't take advantage of that moment, you will give in to the pressures.

Building resilience is not a one-time thing; you don't build it once and move on. You've got to keep working on it because you will have more moments in your life where you will need to be resilient. Like your muscles when you exercise, you need to continue to stretch them to be strong enough for whatever muscle-related activity you will need to do. This realization is why some people feel resilient at a heightened level in their life and feel less so at another level.

Keep building resilience. You must stay committed to the process—learn, unlearn, and relearn. By doing this, you will reshape your mindset to suit the power of being resilient.

How to Build a Resilient Mindset

Develop a Sense of Purpose

First, you've got to develop a sense of purpose! To create a resilient mindset, you need to know where you are headed and why you are going that way. You need to know your goals and what you want to achieve. With a set goal before you, you will see what you are aiming for and you will be able to go for it with a committed focus to see it come to fruition.

People with a sense of purpose don't have time for doubts, fear, or even uncertainty; they know what they want to achieve and develop the resilient mindset to see it through to the end.

What Does Resilience Mean?

When talking about resilience, we should not compare one person to another. As a family member or friend, we need to recognize each person for who they are as an individual and be good listeners.

When going through adversity or internal issues, instead of thinking, "My friend is just so much more resilient than me," we should ask ourselves, "How can I be like that too?"

Think of it as bouncing like a ball rather than

breaking like an egg under pressure. Suicide, for example, is someone breaking. They have been broken to the point that they have lost all hope. So, resiliency, in the simplest terms, is not about being perfect but about becoming better, responding positively to negativity and getting back up after you have been knocked down. Being resilient doesn't mean that you will not experience hardships, trauma, or pain. It means developing the behaviors, actions, and thoughts to grow resilience. It may take time to develop, but you can do it—it's not something that you either have or don't have. Everyone has it! Resilience is a skill, and like all skills, it can be improved.

Learn Not to Feel Like a Victim

People often feel like victims when faced with a drastic change, but this shouldn't be the case. Having a victim mentality obstructs the plans you have to develop a resilient mindset. Instead of acting like someone who has been victimized by the universe, how about we bounce like a ball and brace for the changes that would occur going forward? An oppressed mind will never be a resilient one. This idea is essential. Too many people miss out on living their best lives after military service because they feel like victims.

An example is my dear brother Patrick, my mother's second child after me. His nickname is Patty Duke. He served twenty-two years in the Army. He was a sergeant first class on his second tour in Iraq when the Humvee he was driving on a military transition team got hit with an improvised explosive device in October 2007. He had just one month remaining in his tour.

As you can imagine, this time was extremely frightening for my family and me. When I received the call saying an IED attack had hit my younger brother, I didn't know if he was alive or dead. In a blind panic, I called around to the contacts I had to find out his status. The response I eventually received was "He is fine. He is in the hospital in Landstuhl, Germany, smiling, telling the nurses to stop worrying so much."

Phew. Wait, how is he smiling after such an ordeal? I thought.

Patrick was later transported to Walter Reed Army Medical Center in Washington, DC. I immediately drove down to visit him, and another one of my best friends from the Army community, retired First Sergeant Kevin Cummings, met me at the hospital for support.

I remember being uncharacteristically emotional and running into his room. As I rushed the door, Patrick said, "I'm fine! It's only my foot. I have another. At least they didn't get my hands, or else I wouldn't be able to fish anymore!" We both broke into laughter! He amazed me. He was not upset or frightened that he now had to have a prosthetic limb. He embraced it and didn't for one second let this experience change his powerful mindset.

Develop Problem-Solving Skills

You can develop and maintain a resilient mindset by developing problem-solving skills, which will be helpful as you try to navigate the transition from one phase of your life to another. Some problem-solving skills include analytical skills, innovative and creative thinking skills, and even resilience. Problem-solving skills will empower you with the mental capacity needed to tackle any adjustments you may need to do in any particular situation in life.

Manage Your Emotions

To manage one's emotions means to choose when and how to express them. Sometimes, while on the brink of a transition, we become overly emotional. Our emotions can take over, making us doubtful and frightful of the future. Feelings can also make us do or say things we might regret. Hence, there is a need to learn how to understand, accept, and healthily regulate emotions.

Those who struggle with their emotions are easily swayed by how they feel, forgetting that feelings are changeable. One minute you are sad, and within the hour, you are not. So why build your mind on such an unstable experience? Don't let fear, frustration, and anger get the best of you to the point where you cannot take bold steps. Instead, focus on building a tough mindset by managing your emotions, being intentional with decision making, and facing the transition process head-on.

Surround Yourself with Resilient People

We adopt the energy and vibration of those around us. If you are always around resilient people, you will gradually start to develop resilience. If you are constantly surrounded by people who easily give up, you will do the same.

There is power in association, and you aren't different from the people you spend time with, so pay attention to the people around you. Are they resilient, or do they easily give up? Are they consciously making an effort, or are they rather lazy?

Don't lie to yourself while evaluating the people around you; your honesty is needed at this time. Don't stay connected to relationships that don't help you get better in life. It is YOUR transition, and what you do now will determine how well this happens. Our relationships should help us thrive, not be toxic to us. The more we are surrounded by resilient people, the more we will exude the same resilience.

Know How to Respond to Change

The best way to respond to change is by embracing it and finding the positive attributes of your life. If you always resist change and deal with skepticism, you will have a fragile mindset.

Change strengthens you and keeps you on your toes because you are not always in your comfort zone. No one becomes resilient by being in a comfortable spot, without hardships or challenges to overcome. Change is good. Think about the seasons we experience; there is a time for winter, spring, autumn, and summer. If you don't know how to adapt to these changing seasons, you will struggle with each season.

Do the Hard Things

Resilience is about being mentally tough, focused enough to take the challenges head-on, doing the hard things. This entails making decisions that may initially seem too difficult.

Every time you do the hard things, take the more challenging route, or do something you thought was very tough, you build up your resilience, strengthening your mind. People run away from complicated things because they feel they are not prepared for it, but here is the truth: If you consistently wait to be ready, you will never get anything done.

Sometimes preparations for the next big thing occur amid the battle; as you act on what you should do and make the tough decisions, you train yourself for resilience.

Challenge Your Assumptions

We all have assumptions that we have internalized because of past experiences or based on what we've seen play out in society. For example, there are general assumptions that veterans have a lower chance of succeeding after getting out of military service. This assumption became popular when people saw how some veterans struggled with life after service.

But I have shared my success story with you, proving that this assumption is not correct. Yes, veterans do struggle, just like everyone else. But they also have a chance at succeeding, just like everyone else. So, if you have certain assumptions you've been holding on to, please challenge them, and if they are incorrect, unlearn them.

These false assumptions, if not corrected, can hinder you from having a resilient mindset. Imagine a veteran who believes that he would fail on a large scale; he would become terrified of taking risks post-military. Sometimes assumptions are dangerous—be mindful of them.

One of the best ways to challenge your negative

assumptions and thoughts is through meditation.[1] Despite what people think, meditation is not the process of changing who you are as a person. It is a set of techniques that can help a person reach a state of awareness and focused attention. This is necessary to acknowledge thoughts, both positive and negative, for motivation and resilience.

Research has proven that meditation has psychological advantages. Some of these include reduced stress, increased self-awareness, improved emotional well-being, greater empathy, and improved mindfulness.

With meditation, you can acknowledge your assumptions and identify the reasons for these assumptions. Once you have established what they are and where they come from, you can start debating these negative thoughts and develop a more positive outlook.

Let's go back to the assumption that veterans have a lower chance of survival as civilians. As you think about this concept, you may feel stressed, afraid, or demotivated to push further. But try to meditate on it. Choose a quiet spot, take deep breaths, and focus on your thoughts.

What do you think are the reasons people fail in their transition to civilian life? Then ask yourself: Am I going to do the same? What do I have that they did not? Perhaps because you have a guide, you have an idea of where to start, and it's up to you if you're going to try your best and apply what you learn. Think that you have every key to make your transition smooth. So, it's unlikely for you to fail.

Keep Pushing and Growing

Lastly, you've got to keep on pushing and growing even in the face of setbacks. I know what it feels like to step into another phase of your life with so much uncertainty and thoughts such as "What if this doesn't work out?" But when you have those questions, remember that backing down is not the answer.

The more persistent you become with the process, the easier it gets to build a resilient mindset. As you consistently push, you will stretch the capacity of your mind to take on more pressure, crush it, and win.

Certain things are needed to enable the resilient transition process, and having a resilient mindset is crucial. Can you successfully build a house without a foundation? Of course not! Now think of a resilient mindset as a foundation for resilient transitions. If you get it right, you will do just fine!

The steps in this chapter will help you build a resilient mindset for ALL seasons! Just start with the same steps at different transition phases and remember to remain positively driven.

The next chapter and subsequent sections will

focus more on the attributes and strategies you need to embrace resilient transitions as well as potential pitfalls.

We will talk about how to take charge of your vibration (how you feel), be aware of yourself and others, and take control of your mindset.

6

SEND POSITIVE VIBES TO GET POSITIVE RESULTS

From this chapter onward, you will be exposed to practical and effective steps you can take toward ensuring a smooth transition from one stage of your life to another. First, you've got to believe that you are a vibrational being and that you can send positive vibes.

Why is this idea of being vibrational so essential? Well, it is important because everything in life is a vibration! Music is a vibration that is translated by your ears through the air. Everything that you see and touch is vibrating at the subatomic level. But even your thoughts and feelings are a form of vibration.

We don't see the vibrations around us, but you will feel it if you are conscious of life. You feel that pull toward the things you spend time thinking about and discussing. Everyone vibrates a particular frequency, and the lower the frequency, the denser your energy levels and the heavier your challenges.

A higher vibration would help you remain energized as you go through specific issues. The higher you vibrate, the more confident and stronger you will feel. When you vibrate low, you will feel depressed and defeated.

Vibration is the reason why you feel either confident and strong or depressed and defeated.

Every topic in your life has a vibrational frequency that you give it, such as your health, your wealth, and your relationships. For example, suppose you think about money and it gives you stress. In that case, the subject of money for you has a low vibration. However, if the thought of money makes you feel hopeful and excited, then it has a higher vibration. But you have total and absolute vibrational control over every topic there is. And you have the choice to consciously take control of your thinking process and to purposely think a better-feeling thought or a worse one.

In other words, you have control over how you vibrate or feel by the thoughts you choose to have.

Have you ever met someone, and after a few minutes of talking to them, you felt drained? You probably got back home thinking, "I don't think I want to hang out with this person anymore." You felt that way because of the person's vibrations, which were negatively driven and adversely impacted your energy levels.

This understanding of vibration also explains why we are often advised to pay attention to how people make us feel and who we spend time with. Some people are not even aware that they possess exceptionally low vibrations. If we are unconscious of how it affects us, we can easily be negatively affected.

Remember, you are in charge of your vibrations, and you can choose to boost them by being intentional and sending positive vibes. It is crucial that when you attain a high vibrational level, you strive to maintain it and not allow it to drop because when the levels fall, you become vulnerable to negative experiences.

When you are going through a transition, you experience different emotions. You may be sad about what you're leaving behind, but also excited or anxious about what the future holds. You may have mixed feelings about spending more time with the family. You may be worried about financial matters. You may be relieved about not being required to do certain things anymore like waking up so early to do PT, but then you also miss it and sometimes may even be frustrated at the lack of discipline of the people around you. You may feel over-whelmed by the many options suddenly available to you. You may be happy that no one needs anything from you, and you may be sad that no one needs anything from you.

The range of emotions activated during this period sets the condition for how we feel about the next phase during our transition. This is the basis for the vibration (feelings) we send out to others. A person excited about the next stage of his life, pumped up with enthusiasm and has positive expectations, will operate at a higher vibration. Likewise, a person frightful of changes, unsure and nervous, will emit lower vibrations.

As someone keen on making resilient transitions, I had to ensure that my vibration remained high to make an easier transition from military to post-military life. But this is not the case for everyone. Some people struggle with vibrations and their energy levels; hence, they may be at a high level today and low tomorrow.

When I first got out of the military, I went to a basketball game in West Point with my family. It was a college basketball game. We happened to arrive there late, so we had to sit on the visitors' side instead of West Point's side, which was our home team.

The game was going well; our team was winning, but the visitors were starting to make a good comeback and were attempting some shots. A man and a young boy, who seemed to be father and son, were sitting right in front of me. They stood up to cheer their team, blocking my view entirely of the basketball game. Instinctively, I got very irritated and angry, and I quickly shouted at them, "SIT DOWN! I CAN'T SEE, SIT DOWN!"

The little boy turned around and looked at me with an expression on his face like I was a big, bad monster. And I realized what had just happened: I scared the little boy and embarrassed my family.

As I sat there, I thought I must do something. I have to apologize for this and say sorry to these people. So in that moment, I chose to send a positive vibe after I had verbally transmitted a negative vibe. I told them that I had just gotten out of the military and I hadn't had all of that stuff out of my system yet. I asked them to forgive my inappropriate conduct and told the boy to never act the way I'd acted.

That was one of those moments where I corrected myself. I recognized my mistake and immediately improved myself. This is what I mean with these vibes. Sometimes you have to humble yourself and say, "I am sorry," then let it go.

Maintaining a high vibe is challenging, but the truth is, you can do it! Decide to keep a high vibration until it happens, from the moment you wake up until the moment you go to sleep again. Keeping your feelings positive helps you stay optimistic, with hope, certainty, and assurance that everything will be okay.

Everything in life is composed of energy, which varies in quantity and quality. The kind of vibrations you have can influence how you use the law of attraction, which we will talk more of in Chapter Thirteen.

High vibrations are linked to feelings such as love, compassion, positivity, peacefulness, and light. On the contrary, low vibrations are linked to sadness, depression, anxiety, fear, and uncertainty. If you have exceedingly high vibrations, you will function authentically to get the things you want. When you get what you want, you will manifest from a level of certainty where you attract what you need.

However, when you operate at a lower frequency,

your senses cannot see beyond the challenges. Instead of finding ways to ensure easy and smooth transitions, you feel overwhelmed with emotions, with your mind telling you that you won't make it.

Before we talk about how you can heighten your vibrations with positive vibes and other ideas, we need to understand how low vibrations occur. We also need to learn how to identify low vibrations.

It's okay to feel negative feelings, but we shouldn't allow it to fester to the point that it becomes your frequency. For example, instead of holding on to your anger, forgive. Anger will cause you also to feel other negative emotions, such as bitterness, disappointment, and even regret. But a person who accepts that they are angry and subsequently forgives is free from the trap of harmful vibration and enters a higher frequency.

Resilient transitions are only possible when we operate from positivity, which is possible through a higher vibration. Let's talk about why people have low vibration and how you can tell if you've got one.

Low Vibration and Its Negative Implications

You Feel a Lack of Direction

During the transition phase, you want to feel like you are moving and making progress. But if you feel like you are stuck in one place, paralyzed with ideas and not knowing what to do next, you are operating at a lower frequency.

You Feel Tired

We all feel physically tired sometimes, especially when we have taken on a whole lot at one time, but that is not the tiredness we're talking about right now. We are talking about mental and emotional exhaustion, making a person feel like life is not heading anywhere.

If you are always uninspired, too tired to plan your next move, or apprehensive about the future, then your vibration is low. You need to start feeling inspired and strengthened again to boost that vibration and make you mentally and psychologically prepared for the transition.

You Don't Know What Life Has to Offer You

Some people might say, "But we all don't know what life has to offer, as life is a mystery." The answer is simple: We can shape our lives and know what to expect through our thoughts and energies. While you cannot predict everything about your life, you should be able to hold on to certain assurances that you are on the right path. You need to be optimistic and hopeful, expecting positive things to come your way. If you are not intentional about this, you will be open to all sorts of experiences, including negative ones.

You Feel Stressed about Your Situation

If all you can think about are negative ideas about what is to come, you will have negative experiences. Since energy drives our world, we cannot afford to allow negative energy to move our experiences because what we allow becomes our reality. If you allow negative thought processes to thrive in your mind regarding the transition phase, you will always struggle.

You Struggle to See the Beauty in Life

Those with low vibrations struggle to see and appreciate the beauty in life. Their lower and negative vibes make them feel like there are so many issues in their lives that there is no room for positivity.

If you don't have room for some light and positivity, the struggles in your life will cause you to feel like everyone and everything are against you.

You cannot think this way and expect to go through resilient transitions; you will be at a low vibrational level, which means you will be unsure about what the future holds for you.

You Feel Unprepared

A person has low vibrations and negative vibes if they feel unprepared whenever there is a transition, even after going through rigorous preparation processes.

You've attended all the lectures, studied diligently, even gotten additional support from your teachers, yet you still feel unprepared for the examination. Think of the transition phase as an examination you must pass to move from one level to another. You need to feel prepared to take the exam confidently.

Constantly feeling unprepared and insecure despite all the steps you've taken to prepare means there is a problem with your vibes. That problem needs to be handled for you to experience resilient transitions.

The ideas above are some examples of how you may feel when your vibration is low. Simply put, you feel down for whatever reason. The good news is, yes, you can transform low vibrations into positive and higher vibrations. There are simple techniques you can deploy to get rid of such limiting beliefs and negative energy. Let's find out how you can enable a higher vibration through the power of positive vibes.

High Vibrations and the Power of Positive Vibes

Be Optimistic about the Present and the Future

Optimism and positive vibes work together, so if you want to function at a high vibration, you've got to be optimistic about today and tomorrow. We must emphasize "today" because most people focus on being confident eventually in the future, but what about today?

Whatever you feel and believe about today will affect how you perform in the future. Therefore, optimism shouldn't be solely expressed for the future. When you wake up, get that optimism boost for the day by intentionally getting things done. That is how you work your way up into an optimistic future.

Rise Above the Challenges

Amid the challenges, those with higher vibrations refuse to allow such situations to get the best of them. We must try to rise above the challenges we face because this is how you will learn to maintain a high vibration.

Showing up every day with a negative mindset, sad countenance, and a defeatist mentality only worsens things. But showing up ready to win and break down the walls in front of you keeps you in a positive state of mind until the problems give way to answers.

Be Full of Inspiration

Those with positive and empowering vibrations are always full of inspiration. Such individuals also have their particular challenges but would rather find solutions instead of wallowing in self-pity.

If you don't know how to be inspired, start by

finding what excites you. What are you passionate about? What have you always liked to do but never had the chance or the time to do so? What do you find interesting?

Find inspiration in the little things, and your vibration will remain high.

Find Ways to Lift Others

Those who function at a high vibration are vital pillars of support to other people, and they always find ways to lift them. Some people would instead focus on themselves; hence, they feel overwhelmed by their problems.

Let us give encouragement instead of criticism. Dale Carnegie[1] said, "Abilities wither under criticism; they blossom under encouragement." Each of us has the magic power to empower others simply by generously bestowing praise and showing encouragement rather than criticism to help them recognize their potential.

We should also be sincere as sincerity helps people feel appreciated. If we are sincere, others will also pick up on this and reciprocate it, fostering mutual trust.

It is possible to feel less overwhelmed when you are out looking for different ways to empower and uplift others. My writing this book is a way for me to uplift you and other people who may be finding life transitions very difficult. Think about ways you can help others and you will be working at a higher vibration in life.

People Naturally Open Up to You

Everything around us functions based on our energy and the vibration we emit, so people will find it difficult to open up to you if they feel negative vibes. But on the flip side, if you have positive vibes, people will find you trustworthy and open up to you because they feel and sense that you are positively driven. We are all attracted to positive energy, but beyond that, we also need to become positive energy sources to others. Do the people around you open up to you, or would they instead go somewhere else for advice?

Maximize All Opportunities

An individual keen on maximizing all opportunities is operating at a high vibration. They know that wherever they are is only temporary and they are gearing up to be catapulted to a new height. Hence, they grab all opportunities because they believe in themselves.

Those operating at a lower vibration see opportunities as challenges. This may be why a fresh graduate from college may feel like getting a job is a good option because college is "stressful." But getting that job is an opportunity to gain experience, and someone with positive vibes would take it seriously.

It is not too late to boost your energies and vibrations such that you only emit positive vibes even in a transitory phase. Pay attention to how you feel about your life and how people feel around you. If you discover that you need to implement changes, then do it.

Now you understand the power of your vibrations and the role it plays in enabling you to transition smoothly from one phase of your life to another. Work on your frequencies by always ensuring that you have and give out positive vibes so you can enjoy a smooth transition. Your worries, anxiety, fears, and uncertainties about the next phase shouldn't cause you to feel so down that it affects your vibrations. Be mindful of your emotions, take a pause and work to re-energize your vibrations through music, meditation, a walk in the park, or anything else that brings you calm and peace. Be intentional with enabling positive vibes, and you will enjoy the thrill of a resilient transition.

Next, we will talk about the concept of self-awareness, how you can be conscious of others, and how this relates to a smooth transition.

7

BE AWARE OF YOURSELF AND YOUR IMPACT ON OTHERS

When you function at a very high vibrational level, you become aware of yourself and other people. That awareness helps you understand your unique journey: where you are right now, where you are headed, and what you hope to achieve. Some people have no self-awareness; hence, they don't have a complete understanding of what's happening to them.

Without self-awareness, you are just allowing life to happen to you and you are not in control of the situation. Are you conscious of the things happening to you? Do you feel like you are in charge of your trajectory, or are you only willing to accept whatever happens to you?

Who are you, and why are you at this turning point? What is the essence of your existence, and where are you headed? Do you know your purpose and what you want, or are you leaning on what others expect from you?

Most of the time, we define our identity based on society's definitions, who we are to our friends and family, or our needs. So, it is easier to be aware of our roles as military officers, students, parents, and so on, than of our own identity. If you don't know who you are, the world will dictate that to you, which means you lose yourself daily trying to live up to others' expectations.

You may be struggling with this transition because you're not very conscious of who you are and you don't understand your feelings, so you're having a hard time creating the kind of life you want. Maybe you've always leaned on your parents, spouse, friends, or even mentors to help you navigate life, but here you are at a crossroad, wondering how the next phase of your life will be.

If you are unsure about who you are, you will also lack confidence in making certain decisions. I had to also work on my self-awareness level when I needed to make tough decisions. This has helped me arrive at this unique stage in my life.

Self-awareness is critical because it helps you better understand yourself. It helps you understand why you are concerned about the future and why you don't know what to do next. When you know these whys, it becomes easier for you to solve your problems. You can make changes to your thought process. You can improve in areas that require improvements when you are self-aware.

Through self-awareness, you become conscious of

your strengths and bank on them instead of being unsure. When you are uncertain about your strengths, you wouldn't know what to leverage to make the next phase of your life a productive one. So, you end up doing what other people do because you assume that *might* be good.

When you don't know who you are, you live life by default. In other words, instead of deciding for yourself what job to have or where to live, you simply follow the crowd and do what everyone else does. Too many people are lost in this world because they have not found their purpose, and we need to deal with this challenge before we can make any progress with our transitions.

Understanding Ourselves and Others

The concept of self-awareness also helps us become conscious and aware of others. After all, for you to understand others, you first need to understand yourself. The transitions we experience are never in isolation; they always involve other people. Whenever people are involved, we need to understand their positions and their unique attributes.

Understanding other people helps us realize that all our journeys are different. We don't need to have the exact expectations or experiences to relate to one another. This idea also helps us become authentically true to ourselves instead of living and aligning our life's adventures with other people's plans.

For example, suppose you have a close friend who is also in the military. You both are about to transition from the military to civilian life. In that case, it is common to discuss your plans after service. You both would want to know the path each of you would take, and while that is pretty normal, it can have adverse effects on you if you are not aware of your friend's uniqueness.

Let's say your friend has very distinct ideas about what they want to do, and it seems like your friend's plans are on the extreme. It even sounds like your friend is willing to take significant risks that you usually wouldn't do.

If you are not self-aware and not conscious of who your friend is, you may also become tempted to model your post-military life after your friend's plans. When you do this, you may enter a season of struggles, fears, anxiety, and ultimately give up because you can't handle the risks your friend is willing to take. On the other hand, your friend flourishes and thrives because they are on their path and doing exactly what they want to do.

When you become aware of others, you develop a deep appreciation for who they are and their authenticity. You encourage them to stay true to themselves without putting pressure on them.

It's okay to gain inspiration from someone else, but

there is a big difference between inspiration and imitation. People who imitate often struggle because they try to fit a square into a circle—they are being inauthentic. On this transition journey, you must stay true to yourself by first knowing who you are and knowing who others are.

Understand that your next moves will vary according to your priorities in life. Some people may want to work on their families, while others may want to work on their careers. Different people will plan their transitions differently based on their values, priorities, and goals.

If you are family oriented, you must understand and be aware of the career-oriented person. You don't have to change your values or priorities just because you feel like they are doing better than you.

Being aware of others also means being less judgmental of people's choices when they may not seem right to you. Maybe after school, the normal process entails getting a job first, but here you are with your best friend who is keen on starting a business and taking the entrepreneurial route. If you are supportive of your friend, you won't chastise that decision, nor would you try to copy him and become entrepreneurial yourself (if you are not ready for it). Your friend has their path, and you also have yours. Your friend would flourish as an entrepreneur, and you would thrive doing your own thing as an employee building a robust work experience.

How to Become Self-Aware

Spend Time with Yourself

Enjoy your alone times, as these are moments through which you can reflect, understand your motives, and be at peace with your truth. Spending time with yourself can be by meditating, exercising, journaling, even going for a walk!

Listen to Your Inner Voice

Our inner voice always prompts us to get things done or helps us make decisions; this is our internal guidance system. Don't ignore your inner voice, as it can be very instrumental in helping you figure out your life. Most people listen to everyone else but that inner voice. Hence, they feel conflicted when they need to make decisions while in transition.

Clarify Your Values

What are your values? Do you know the things you can never compromise? If you want to become self-aware, you need to clarify your values. Know what you stand for; this is how you can thrive as an authentic individual.

Know Your Strengths and Weaknesses

We all have those areas we excel in and those we need to improve in. Know these areas, and you will become self-aware. Don't try to ignore your weaknesses because you are embarrassed by them. Your weaknesses are signs that you can still improve your life. Embrace all of you and bask in the thrill of living an authentic life.

Understand the Trajectory of Your Life

Self-awareness is also possible when you start understanding the trajectory of your life: where you are from, your present reality, and where you are going. These three components constitute your life's journey, and it is a great starting point for self-awareness.

How to Become Aware of Others

Be an Active Listener

We communicate who we are through our conversations. If you listen well enough, you will have an idea of who they are, which will help you become more accepting. Always listen with the intent to understand and not just to give a reply.

When you listen actively, you not only consider the meaning of the words but also see the meanings of their body language and other non-verbal cues. This is vital to building connections with others. Some active listening techniques include asking for clarifications, summarizing, asking questions, eye contact, and listening with a neutral and non-judgmental viewpoint. These techniques will help you achieve a deeper understanding of the conversation and help you build trust and rapport with other people.

Accept People

This idea is crucial as we live in a world where people are encouraged to change through channels such as social media platforms and become what the majority deems "acceptable." But we strip people of their authenticity and remain oblivious of who they are when we don't accept them.

Everyone cannot be like you, and everyone shouldn't be like you! So learn to accept people and value them for who they are instead of trying to change them. If you feel they can do better in certain areas, make your suggestions without being forceful and demeaning.

Respect Others' Values

We've also got to respect people's values to be truly aware of them. We have our values, and we expect other people to respect our values when relating with us, so we should do the same for others. When we respect their values, it becomes easier for us to be aware of them and accept them. People's transitions will mirror their values. Even if your friends' values are something you do not believe in, openly listen and learn why they feel this way.

Communicate When Uncertain

If you are uncertain about a particular idea or feeling about a person, ask questions and communicate your uncertainty. Sometimes we fail to become aware of others when we make assumptions about them without seeking clarity. People will show you their true selves when you ask. If you don't "get" them, communicate with them. You may need some time to process your thoughts and feelings; take all the time you need to figure out what might be making you think or feel a certain way. Recognizing specific triggers and feelings is the first step to changing them.

Be Supportive

You can be more aware of other people by being supportive when they share their plans and dreams. Don't try to change their plans because it is something you wouldn't do. That shows a lack of awareness about who they are, and you need to do better with being supportive. The more supportive you are, the better you can accept others and be supportive of their plans.

We can achieve a resilient transition and enjoy the process. But we must know who we are and understand others. We cannot maximize the benefits of resilient transitions by modeling our lives after other people's plans or achievements. Be inspired by others, but don't make your life goals all about them. Be true to yourself, know who you are, and place some value on your life decisions. Decide that you would make the best out of every situation regardless of what happens. With this mindset, nothing can stop you.

8

UNIVERSITY LIFE AFTER MILITARY SERVICE

Many service members choose to go back to school after leaving the military. On top of adjusting to your civilian status, and COVID-19, navigating university life and campus life can be very challenging.

This chapter explores how we can have resilient transitions as we go to college for the first time or after graduating. Although the ideas here have been made through the lens of a veteran, they also can apply to everyone. If you are not a veteran or a student, don't worry. You could still find the lessons I will unveil empowering.

Difficulties in Academic Transitions

Many students go to college thinking they would make lots of friends, have a thriving social life, and have a great time. Sometimes, these expectations happen, but when they do not, they lead to feelings of loneliness.

Students leave home, travel for many miles, leave the supportive embrace of their friends and family to go to a new environment that is sometimes too fast-paced for them. Soon enough, they feel homesick, awkward, and isolated.

These experiences are all normal. It is also normal for the veteran to feel isolated after getting back from the military. And it is normal for an employee to feel stressed after returning to the office after working from home for many months because of COVID-19.

Students feel the weight of this enormous change, and even when they try to adjust, the adjustment process can be draining. They now have to adjust to new lifestyles, new study demands, and new experiences, as well as cope with more significant responsibilities, pressures, and expectations.

Some students find it helpful to go home more frequently, but for others, going home is not the answer, so they stay "stuck" along with their feelings. The feelings they hold also make it difficult for them to participate in social activities or become assertive. If you're currently a student, you probably could relate to some if not everything I've shared so far, right?

No one stays a freshman forever, so you will be able to adjust eventually, but the quality of your experiences will be determined by how you handle this initial transition.

This phase is not the time to cry, allow anxiety to creep in, or become isolated. This time right now is precious and one that ends quickly. Before you know it, you are almost done with school, and you want to look back with fond memories.

How to Deal with Pressure

Pressure can come from all sides. There is pressure that builds up from within. There is pressure from society, from people around us. You put pressure on yourself to succeed; you want to conquer the world and have a successful career.

Students graduate from college and feel they need to impress everyone and show that their years in school weren't a waste of time. There's pressure to create a new structure for yourself as the university system no longer exists. You have to start structuring your time, the access you give people to get into your life, and everything about your life in general.

Pressure also comes from the desire to make new friends and connect with new people because after graduation you and your friends might have gone your separate ways.

And then there are financial pressures. Nobody tells you about the pressure you feel about paying bills, loans, and taking care of yourself, which means you've got to get a job and excel at it.

New graduates also beat themselves up a lot

because they feel like they are failures when they get numerous job application rejections. Ah, rejections! That could feel like everyone is saying NO to you all the time, all at the same time.

These challenges we just covered that relate to both students and graduates are REAL. They threaten their transition process. But since the challenges are never-ending and part of the experience, we've got to find ways to reinvent the wheel and be inspired despite the obstacles.

The big question is, "How can students navigate and adjust to university life, and how can graduates ensure a smooth transition?" Let's find answers, shall we? We will begin with the students; I will show you how to make easy adjustments to your new university life. Then we will focus on the new graduates and how to successfully transition from university life to the real world.

How to Adjust to University Life

For any student to experience resilient transitions from preschool days all through university life, they need to know how to adjust appropriately. Adjusting doesn't mean you wouldn't have initial struggles; it means that you are determined and persistent in your resolve to thrive as a student despite the challenges. Here is how you can adjust to university life.

Build Emotional Strength

You might have heard people say, "Just control what you feel." But if they only knew what you had been through, they would have known that that's easier said than done. No one can truly control what they feel because it is a by-product of specific stimuli from the environment. We can only build emotional strength so we express our emotions more healthily and appropriately.

Building emotional strength[1] is a relatively new way to respond to one's emotions. It involves being vulnerable to the intense emotional experience to express it constructively to prevent outbursts.

Yale Center for Emotional Intelligence has developed the RULER[2] approach to build emotional intelligence skills. It stands for

- RECOGNIZE your emotions
- UNDERSTAND the causes
- LABEL your emotions
- EXPRESS your emotions
- REGULATE your emotions

First, you need to recognize and accept your feelings regardless of how problematic they may be. Accept that you feel lonely, isolated, and even awkward; whatever you feel, own it, and accept that it is a common experience for all freshmen.

Don't ignore or underplay your feelings as this is

self-denial and you won't achieve anything from it. You will be living in denial, and you will not be working on those feelings.

Then you need to understand the source. What are the triggers of these emotions? When you identify what causes them, you can either bring yourself to terms with it or avoid it, depending on how severely the trigger affects you.

The third step is to label it. It's not enough to say, "I feel bad." You need to put a specific label on it so you can further understand what you feel. If needed, label it and further describe it. For example, "I feel anxious. My heart is beating fast."

Next is to express your emotions. For example, communicate what you feel to the person who offended you. Make them understand why their actions offended you. This way, they will know better and be empathetic, especially to other people who have been through the same as you.

After these steps, you could better regulate them. If you're in a social situation, excuse yourself for a bit and get some fresh air. You can go for a walk or jog. Some even draw, do yoga, meditate, write in a journal, and get into martial arts. I prefer listening to music to regulate my emotions. But you can always use a combination of ways, especially when these can help you cool down.

So, you see, accepting your feelings helps you become bold and courageous to show up every day ready to win. You will be saying, "Yes, I feel tired and frustrated because there is so much to do, but no, I won't allow that feeling to get the better of me."

Be Intentional with Self-Management

Being intentional is essential! This means having the right mindset and discipline to prioritize your goals. In other words, have good self-management skills. Despite what people think, self-management does not only entail accomplishing your daily goals, but it also allows you to grow in other realms such as physical, mental, social, and spiritual.

Sometimes students struggle to adjust because they don't manage their time effectively. Hence, they feel school is too fast-paced for them. They cannot keep up with the timetables or meet project deadlines, and they struggle with other extra-curricular activities. Furthermore, students no longer have time to exercise, achieve a balanced diet, take care of spiritual needs, and socialize with others. All these are essential to all human beings.

This problem can be solved with intentional self-management skills. You need to know what is expected of you and plan how you intend to get things done. When you schedule your time, you also avoid the pitfalls of procrastination and doing things at the last minute.

Find a Support Network

We need people to help us adjust to any new experience, so you need new friends—even better, a good support network. While nurturing the friendships you had at home can be heartwarming, try to seek ways to find new friends on campus—not just any friend, but a friend who is willing to understand your history and your present mindset. Many people find it difficult to adjust to veterans' beliefs, personalities, and temperaments because of the scars and trauma of war. This is why you need to find friends who can understand what you feel and your triggers. With their support, you can build emotional resilience in school. You will feel more welcome, which can help you adapt to civilian life.

With friends, you wouldn't have to walk alone or constantly feel lonely. You will also have people close to you who are going through the same thing, and together, you all become a support system to one another.

You may think, "But I don't know how to make new friends." Well, start with a kind smile, introduce yourself, get to know the other person, and be interested, courteous, and polite. Keep in touch with your new friend, stay positive, and avoid negative vibes. With friends, you can quickly make adjustments and be fully integrated into the university system.

Enjoy the University Experience

It is imperative to try and enjoy the university experience in order to adjust. That enjoyment starts with having a curious mind about your environment. Be open to visit new places, aim to interact with students who have been in school longer than you, and use your weekends productively to explore.

Enjoy your classes, assignments, and interactive sessions with your instructors and classmates, and spend time getting to know people. By being intentional with enjoying your university experience, you will also become an approachable person who people see as fun, warm, and accepting. With that disposition, you will not struggle with making friends, making your experience even more prosperous.

Explore New Places

You cannot adjust to university life by being stuck in one place. You should become intentional with exploring new places, which will help you acclimate to the university setting.

Share Your Challenges

While exploring new places, remember to share your challenges with others. If you don't have friends yet, find out if your university has a counseling/therapy center where you can interact with a professional counselor. Please don't keep your problems to yourself; share them and get help.

Difficulties in Non-Academic Transitions

The university days prepare you for the kind of career you want, and ideally it should also prepare you for the days after graduation and empower you for "real life" or life out in the real world.

Although when you're done with college you wouldn't have studying times, lengthy assignments, or dissertations anymore, these are replaced by other similarly challenging activities.

Students celebrate their graduation with so much glee and anticipation of what the world has to offer to them. But they get into the real world and are met with the stark truth—the world doesn't offer them anything; the world tries to see what *they* have to offer.

While in school, students were used to most things being planned for them: classes, exam timetable, library time, etc. But after graduation, they must transition into a more independent and unpredictable lifestyle where they own their time and decide what to do with it. Imagine transitioning from a scheduled environment to one where you have so much to do with extraordinarily little time coupled with the pressure to "succeed."

How to Transition from University to Career

Graduating from college often leads to mixed emotions. First, you are excited that school is over, and then you are anxious about the future. You must also deal with uncertainties about the right path to take.

Though challenging, attitude is everything. Choose to get excited because there are many life lessons to be learned from this stage of your life. You will learn every day as you transition, and the ideas below will help ensure you have a smooth one.

Accept Changes

You've done it before, and you can do it again. Accept the changes you experience now that you are no longer in school. Yes, it's a different world, but you can overcome any challenge. Remember that only those who are resilient enough will experience smooth transitions.

Tell yourself, "This is where I am now, and I am going to ensure that it is the most productive experience." Accepting the changes resets your mindset from being a victim and repositions it to take advantage of this moment to improve your life.

Face the hard truths: You are no longer a student! Now look to your future for all the good things to come.

See Life Through an Optimistic Lens

Next, you've got to see your life from this moment on through an optimistic lens and not through a lens of fear, apprehension, and uncertainty. Even if things may not be going your way, it is important to keep your end goal in mind and stay optimistic. Try not to avoid things or experiences that may bring you joy. It helps to be around people who feel safe and upbeat. Their positive vibes bring more optimism your way. However, being optimistic doesn't mean you shouldn't put in the work!

Have a Get-Up-and-Go Attitude!

While building up optimism, remember to do your best to avoid being a couch potato, waiting and hoping for opportunities. Some new graduates stay home all day, watch movies, go on social media, and remain that way with nothing significant happening in their lives.

It may feel easy to just be lazy but don't give in to it. Get up with a sense of purpose and chase your goals. If you have an excellent day, fabulous! And if you don't, accept the lessons learned and endeavor to have a better one tomorrow.

When They Say No, Push Harder!

When you get out there to seek opportunities, be prepared to get many nos. Even when you feel like you don't deserve it, you will be faced with disappointments, and in those moments, you need to push HARDER!

Take the example of a moving train. Nothing successfully stands in its way. The train keeps moving, and if something shows up, the train knocks it down. If you are a moving train mentally and physically, even when you get a hundred nos, you keep moving forward.

Only those who continue moving forward experience resilient transitions that enable them to dominate new levels.

Avoid Unnecessary Comparisons

You may notice some of your friends from school doing better than you, making you wonder if you are doing enough. Yes, you are. The feeling of competition or discontent is a distraction and unnecessary at this time.

You are on this transition experience trying to outdo YOUR past, not competing with anyone else. You may congratulate and partner up with those who are doing well, but you must keep your eyes on your goals.

Develop Specific Skills

To transition well to life after school, you will need specific skills in demand in the workplace. Decide on the career you want, learn about the necessary skills to succeed in such areas, and train yourself to be excellent at them.

Some people cannot successfully transition because they are not prepared for the workforce or life after school. Preparation gives you an advantage, an edge that makes you valuable, so please take this seriously.

Be Patient and Persevere

Lastly, be patient with your transition. I know you want everything to happen suddenly, and you cannot wait for excellent results, but sometimes these things take time and you've got to persevere.

Patience is a necessary part of the transitioning process. Enduring the process will eventually forge you like gold that gets purified by fire; you will come out refined, shiny, beautiful, and most importantly, valuable.

The university experience is a classic example of why transitions can be challenging. You get into a structured educational system that offers foundational support in terms of activities, timing, and a goal: graduation with a degree. But after four years, that structure disappears and you must fend for yourself. Complaining about what you don't have doesn't change anything; you've got to be resilient in the face of such challenges.

As a student, resilient transition means attending

classes even when you feel awkward and isolated. As a graduate, it means pressing forward when you get multiple rejections. Resilience means showing up regardless of how you feel and doing what needs to be done to advance yourself.

9

MANIFEST YOUR NEW NORMAL

When you are set to transition from one phase in your life to another, you will enter what is described as a "new normal." Your new normal includes the things you will be doing and learning in your new phase and how it will affect your journey. The new normal could be different work schedules, new closing hours, or even a bigger office space.

You can experience a resilient transition with this new normal by manifesting it even before you get into it. If you have heard about the concept of manifesting things and you felt left out because it hasn't worked for you, you are in for a treat. This chapter will teach you all you need to know about manifesting things such that they become natural to you even before they happen.

The manifestation process entails turning all the ideas you have about your new phase into reality. It requires you to take steps toward whatever you desire. Please don't expect it to happen overnight; there is a time for manifesting it. There is also a time for putting in the work so what you manifest happens.

You control many of the things that happen to you through your thoughts, and from that thought realm, you can manifest a lot of things into your current existence.

The following is an example:

Have you ever randomly thought about someone and got a text from the person within the hour? Or maybe you thought about someone, and suddenly, the person calls you or shows up at your door? In those moments, we feel weird thinking, "What just happened?" Well, what happened was that you unintentionally used your mind to manifest that person's presence.

Now, if you did that unintentionally, imagine all you would achieve if you did it intentionally. Think about what else you can do with your life, what else can you manifest. You are powerful. You can do it.

Manifestation also means bringing something tangible into your life through attraction and belief; it will come if you think about it. The manifestation process means making everything you want to feel and experience become your present reality using your emotions, thoughts, actions, and beliefs. The manifestation principle works on several things, from love to money and even your new normal.

Now that you are at this pivotal point where you are about to transition from one phase to another, ask yourself this vital question: What do I want from this new normal?

You've got to know what you desire from the shift happening in your life so you can manifest it. This idea of manifestation also shows that you are not helpless, and you have the power to demand what you want from your life and get it. Sometimes we go through transitions hoping that the process will have something to offer us, but your next phase has nothing to offer. Instead, it is what you make of it that counts; whatever you desire from the new phase can happen if you stick to the manifestation process.

There is no need for apprehension over how the next phase will be because you can rebuild it in your mind and get what you desire. Now let's talk about how to start manifesting your new normal.

Start with Clear Goals

People approach manifestations differently, but the first and most fundamental principle entails obvious goals: What do you want? You are in charge of this process, but you've got to know what you want first.

Knowing what you want in life is essential to accomplish goals and boost your psychological well-being. Researchers have proven that goal setting is crucial for motivation, contentment, and productivity. And you cannot deny that when you feel these things, you feel like you have a sense of purpose. Instead of focusing on negative thoughts, you will be focused on your objectives. As a result, you will be less likely to be defeated by depression, anxiety, and PTSD. Goal setting can also help you curb alcohol or drug misuse.

If you want to set goals effectively, consider the SMART acronym. Your objectives must be Specific, Measurable, Achievable, Relevant, and Time-bound.

When we say something specific, it should be detailed. What do you want in this new normal? What kind of changes do you seek? You know the dreams you wish to attain, so be detailed with those images. Don't just say, "I want a job." What kind of job do you need? Don't say, "I want to start a new business." What type of business do you want? The more detailed you are, the more images you visualize, the more manageable your manifestation will be.

Next, your goals should be measurable. This answers the question of how much or how many? Financial goals, for example. How much do I need for my yearly tuition fees? Or if you want to build your relationships, you can ask, "How many hours do I need to spend with my family to bond with them?"

Your goals should also be achievable. Do not set unrealistic goals, as this will only put more pressure on you. As much as possible, your goals should be achievable within a specific period.

Your goals should be relevant. They should mean

something to you. Otherwise, it's not going to make you happy in the long run.

Lastly, your goals should be time-bound. As mentioned, set a specific period in which to accomplish your goals. Set goals you can achieve in your lifetime.

Ask the Universe for What You Want

After gaining clarity on your goals, you need to start asking the universe for what you want. You can do this in a variety of ways: through prayers, visualization, meditation, getting a vision board, or speaking the intentions aloud. You can also write down your preferences and ensure to read what you write often. Be specific with what you ask for and hold on to the images you create, for this is the pathway through which your manifestations will occur.

Start Visualizing

Now start visualizing and creating clear images of what you want. Have daily times when you think and take pictures of what you want. Next, create a vision board of what you want your future to look like. With those images, you will start to manifest the things you want.

The visualization process should be consistent, intentional, and detailed. Don't work with abstract ideas, and don't visualize only when you feel like it;

you've got to do it regularly, be committed, and you will get the results you seek.

Start Working Toward Your Goals

Manifesting is like co-creating something, so it's a collaborative effort between you and the universe. While the universe works to give you what you are trying to manifest, you also need to work toward getting those things. You will not get results without acting on your goals.

Always set time aside to think about the steps you would take to ensure that your dreams come to fruition. Then, build those steps into a routine and remain consistent.

If you start a new career after military service, start working toward networking with people in that field or take certification courses. If you are still looking for work, practice for your job interviews. Don't leave the universe to do its work alone because, without your input, it wouldn't work.

Be Conscious and Grateful

As you work toward your goals and manifest them, remember to be conscious of what happens to you and remain thankful for the things you have. Don't wait until the big things happen before acknowledging your blessings and expressing gratitude. Gratitude is essential within the concept of manifesting what you want. The more thankful you are, the more things you will manifest. To foster more feelings of gratitude, get a gratitude journal. Before going to bed, spend ten minutes thinking and writing about gratitude. Do this daily, and you will get closer to the things you want to manifest.

Eliminate All Limiting Beliefs

Eliminate all obstacles and limiting beliefs that cloud your vision and prevent you from enjoying the benefits of manifesting all you visualize. For example, stop telling yourself you are not good enough and avoid all forms of negative self-talk.

Yes, you are stepping into a new season of your life, but you are worthy of that season, and you will overcome any challenges in it. Manifest from the position of positivity, and you will always get what you want. Whatever causes you to resist the visions you incorporate into your manifestations should be removed, including negative people.

Always Check and Change Your Energy

Positive energy is everything! The energy you send out into the world is the energy you will get back. If you consistently send out negative energy, you will attract the same negative experiences. As you prepare to transition to the civilian world, your thoughts and feelings must reflect positivity, so always check yourself.

You cannot successfully manifest good things when you are always giving off negative energy. If you want love, money, joy, and progress, you must intentionally give off positive energy. Lift your energy by engaging in activities that cultivate joyful feelings within you.

Manifest the kind of life you want as you resiliently transition. For example, suppose you feel stuck, and nothing is happening in your life despite your efforts. In that case, another option is to invest time in helping others:

- Volunteer for a charity.
- Help a friend.
- Reach out to comfort someone in a difficult time.

You can also focus on how you want to feel. If you want to feel productive and loved, for example, then happily set your heart on thoughts that make you feel that way in order to manifest it.

Upgrade Your Manifestations

When you get what you want at a particular stage, nothing stops you from upgrading your manifestations and approaching a new level. For example, you wanted a job after graduating, so you manifested the kind of job you wanted. Now you want a promotion on that job; instead of worrying how that will happen, use the manifestation process again. You can always upgrade your manifestations to reflect where you are in life and your current needs.

Remember that the "new normal" will not always be new; other events will happen in your life that will overtake that new normal. So always feel free to manifest as your life evolves.

Whatever you've initially achieved can be better; you probably don't think about this because you feel it is too big an ambition. But listen, within the world of manifestations, there are no limitations. So long as you can think and visualize it, you can get it!

Manifest Whatever You Want

Yes, you can! You can visualize and manifest anything you want during your transition. For example, if you wish for money, look at the abundance in your life and express gratitude for it. Even if you are struggling with paying your bills, increase your vibration and eliminate all limiting beliefs. Welcome money into your new routine, envision prosperity coming to you, and focus on what you do have. Don't focus on what you don't have.

If you want new friendships and relationships in your new routine, you can get it. Think about the kind of people you want or need in your life and use the power of your imagination to attract them.

Remember that you cannot talk about manifesting money and sitting idle in your new normal. For example, as a veteran, while manifesting money, you also need to be out there seeking opportunities. Likewise, as a young graduate, if you need new relationships, you also need to be the kind of person you desire in order to physically attract similar people.

Don't Give the Universe Mixed Signals

Next, don't give the universe mixed signals by thinking one thing today and another thing the next day and another thing the day after. Your thoughts and visualizations must be consistent. You must be certain about what you want.

Christmas is such a fun holiday, and children love Santa Claus because they can ask him for anything and believe that they will get it. But if the children keep changing their minds, not sure of what they want, they might end up with nothing. Santa, or their parents, need the list on time.

Just as Santa needs his list from the kids, the universe needs you to be sure of what you need. Do you need a job in a particular place? Do you want a specific kind of increase with your business? Think about these things, contemplate them, and make your visualization process clear.

You need such a sense of certainty to make the manifestation process easier. So, if you are uncertain about what you need, take the time to think about it before starting the visualization process.

Trust Your Manifestation Process

Lastly, you've got to trust the process! Listen, the manifestation process works, but if you doubt it, you will struggle with it. Questioning the manifestation is akin to planting a seed in healthy soil, pulling it out the same day, then planting it and pulling it again. If you keep doing this, the seed will never germinate.

You've got to trust that the seed will one day become a plant or a tree, just like an acorn that becomes an oak tree. So, plant your seeds, water them, and watch them grow! Follow the steps mentioned above, believe in your creative ability, see what you want, and manifest it into the world.

Sometimes, doubt settles in our minds when we are impatient, and as mentioned previously, you cannot afford to be impatient. A transition takes time, and during that time, you must be patient. While waiting, MANIFEST!

I encourage people to read books because of the wealth of knowledge they could grasp through books. You may not know many things because you haven't opened a book that can teach you what you don't know. Some people have heard about these manifestation concepts but haven't maximized them because they don't know how to go about it.

Imagine what impact a book like this could have on their minds and their efforts toward manifesting. You now know how it works. Utilize it as you transition from one stage of life to another.

The question then becomes, what do you want? See it, feel it, and achieve it!

10

USING MUSIC AS THERAPY

In the United States, creative arts therapies are part of Veterans Health Administration (VHA) Recreation Therapy Service and are direct-care programs that include the following disciplines: art therapy, dance/movement therapy, drama therapy, and music therapy. Creative arts therapists are nationally certified clinical professionals who use arts modalities and creative processes to promote wellness and rehabilitation through unique personal interactions. The discipline that has helped me with my transition is music therapy.

Do you have THAT song? You know the one I mean —the one you listen to and it instantly makes you feel better. You sing along, smile, maybe even dance! This is likely your favorite song because you associate a happy memory with it. Its presence enhances your mood within the first few beats. Can you think of that song now? Play it and see how your mood changes. For me it's "Happy" by Pharrell Williams; try it and let me know what you think.

The American Music Therapy Association[1] states that music programs enable stress management through therapeutic measures. In a sudden transition, therapy is often recommended to help an individual move from the past into the present.

In music therapy, music is used as a form of treatment, as it could empower your brain to defend against mood disorders. Since there are no side effects with this therapeutic form, you can always rely on music to uplift you in those uncertain times.

Music evokes emotional strength that helps you face every new day with a renewed hope that things will work out fine for you. As a result, you will sleep better, wake up mentally stronger, and better handle the hurdles that come your way as you make life changes.

Many things that happen to you start as a response in your brain. When you manifest these emotions and feelings in real time, you only react to what goes on in your brain. For example, if you touch a scorching cup of tea, you will instinctively recoil in pain. Why did you pull away? Well, you withdrew your hand because your brain responded to the pain associated with handling a scorching item.

Music also has the same impact on your brain. Knowing how to maximize it will aid your resilient transitional process. Music is a healing tool; it expresses how people feel in a way that the listeners can relate. It is a medium that humans can appreciate in some form or another.

Sometimes when words fail us and we cannot express how we feel, music speaks for us. Music can also create a universal bond, which transcends borders. When someone in the United States releases an album, it can generate millions of streams in other countries regardless if people in those countries can understand English or not connect with the lyrics.

So how can music help us make the requisite changes we need to move from one life stage to another in a positive manner during your transition? Let's find out!

How the Brain Reacts to Music

Studies on the connection between music and the brain have proven that human beings are hard-wired to respond to music. Scientific findings have proven that music assists patients struggling with Parkinson's disease.[2] Furthermore, as music enhances brain function, people struggling with mental illness[3] will experience relief when listening to music.

Various parts of the brain respond to music. Understanding how this works may help encourage you to be intentional in your use of music. Below, we will consider some parts of the brain[4] and what happens to them when listening to music.

Navigating Complex Thought Processes

The corpus callosum enables the right and left hemispheres to effectively communicate, thus allowing for coordinated body movements and helping you navigate complex thought processes. Music aids with this smooth coordination, making it easy for you to stay calm through the process.

Releasing Essential Hormones

The hypothalamus is the part of your brain that keeps your body in balance by linking the endocrine and nervous systems, thus producing and releasing essential hormones. Certain chemicals that regulate our sleep, mood, heart rate, and body are also present in the hypothalamus. If you play a clear sound like Mozart, you will observe that your heart rate and blood pressure start to reduce, helping you stay calm and focused during the transition process.

Navigating Numerous Emotional Reactions

The hippocampus produces and retrieves memories while regulating emotional responses and helps us navigate numerous emotional reactions. If you are confused or feeling lost as you navigate your transition, you need to listen to soothing music.

When you listen, the sounds from the music will

increase neurogenesis in the hippocampus, thus allowing you to produce new neurons that also improve your memory.

Triggering Emotions

The amygdala is a part of the brain that processes and triggers emotions. For example, music can help you with fear control and also prepares you to enjoy pleasure. Whenever you listen to music and feel shivers down your spine, your amygdala is getting activated. You need that experience to stay calm while you transition.

Releasing Neurotransmitter Dopamine

The nucleus accumbens seeks pleasure and reward, which plays a huge role in addiction; it releases the neurotransmitter dopamine. Music can also be addictive but that is not a negative thing; it increases dopamine in the nucleus accumbens, and dopamine creates feelings of pleasure that motivate you in this transitional phase.

Storing Physical Memory

The cerebellum coordinates movement and stores physical memory. For example, a patient with Alzheimer's who may not recognize his spouse may still be able to play the guitar due to muscle memory. The memories in your cerebellum do not fade away.

As you transition and time goes on, you don't want to forget the moments and memories that you had in your previous environment. While listening to music, you remember the high points of your previous career or life stage and use those as a stimulant for greatness in the next phase.

I've thought hard about how I succeeded in my military career, getting promoted to sergeant in my first two years of service, then rapidly ascending up the ranks, eventually making it all the way to command sergeant major, the highest enlisted rank. Music was certainly an important part of my life in those days; however, I was not necessarily conscious of the vital role it played or could have played.

When I look back and examine those images of success, I remember how the military cadence made me feel when we were running during basic training. Or the times during the Gulf War when I relied on music like the gospel songs sung by Mrs. Florence Jackson of my Church, St. Marks Baptist in Highland Falls. Or the hip-hop mixtapes that my cousin Doug, aka DJ Trife, from Spring Valley, New York, used to send me.

Music made me believe I could make it through those tough days in combat. So once again I turned to music and it propelled me to believe that I can pull myself out of the darkness of depression and win during my post-military experience as a veteran. It was the turning point, and I began to excel as a leader within my community.

Visualizing Music Scores

The occipital lobe enables us to see. Did you know that professional musicians use this part of the brain (also the visual cortex) when listening to music? Oh yes, they do, while laypersons like us use the temporal lobe (this is the auditory and language center).

This suggests that musicians could visualize music scores when they are listening to the composition. While you may not be a musician, listening to music can help you visualize your next stage.

Analyzing and Enjoying Music

The Wernicke's Area is a part of the brain that aids the comprehension of written and spoken language. We also use this to analyze and enjoy music. Enjoying music means you start to find the little joys in your life again. This is one of the most powerful ways for you to have an easy transition.

Expressing Music

The Broca's Area helps us produce speech, and we use this part of the brain to express music. Playing an instrument, producing sound, improves our ability to communicate better. During the transition stage, some people find it difficult to express themselves, so they bottle up their frightful emotions until they become depressed. But with music, self-expression is easily attained, empowering us to share and speak about our feelings when transitioning from one life stage to another.

Processing What You Hear

Your temporal lobe processes what you hear, and it spans both sides of the brain. We utilize this language center to appreciate music. Language and words are interpreted in the left hemisphere, and music and sounds in the right. As you listen to music, you enhance your hearing processes, making it easier for you to appreciate the depths of music.

Enhancing Decision Making and Planning

The brain's frontal lobe is used during the thinking process and enables the decision-making and planning experience. This frontal lobe is crucial to human beings. Our lobes are more significant than other animals', giving us the increased ability to think, process, and plan. For example, when we listen to music, we enhance the brain's frontal lobe function, making it easier for us to make rapid decisions even when under pressure.

. . .

Now that you know how music impacts the brain, let's build on top of that and consider the top-five ways music can aid resilient transitions.

How Music Aids Resilient Transition

Music Reduces Anxiety

It is common to experience anxiety when transitioning from one life stage to another. Since music has a calm and relaxing effect on the body, anxiety will be a thing of the past. You will find that you are more relaxed, calm, at peace, and mentally prepared to boldly step into a new season of your life. Try a song called "Someone Like You" by Adele to help you relax and reduce anxiety and let me know what you think.

Music Relieves Stress

The transition process induces a lot of stress because you are often worried about the changes you are likely to experience. If you feel stressed out in those moments, listen to your favorite music, and you will feel better. Scientific research[5] reveals that babies remain calmer for longer when they are serenaded by soothing music.

If distressed infants can get relief from music, you

can also have the same results. Music lowers the body's cortisol levels, the hormone released in response to stress. Listening to music can also reduce the heart rate. What works for me is listening to some of my favorite songs that instantly give me positive upbeat vibes like

1. "Let's Go Crazy" by Prince
2. "Walking on Sunshine" by Katrina & The Waves
3. "Tightrope" by Janelle Monáe
4. "Three Little Birds" by Bob Marley & The Wailers
5. "Lovely Day" by Bill Withers

Music Boosts and Evokes Our Memories

Some songs remind us of particular periods, seasons, and events in our lives that make us smile or reminisce on fond memories. I frequently listen to old-school hip-hop for this purpose.

Here is another example. If you are currently in a happy marriage and you plan on moving to a new city, you could be worried about the move because you want to be sure that you will be in a great neighborhood and a great community.

Listening to music played at your wedding ceremony or songs that remind you of your feelings will evoke loving memories of how you both started. This could boost your confidence in you and your partner's decision to move. It could lead you to think that there is nothing you both cannot go through together, which is the true definition of resilient transitions.

Music Creates Optimism

Have you listened to a song and felt like you had super-powers? At that moment, the sounds and musical content have birthed optimism within you such that fear dissipates, and you are set to take the following steps into your new season confidently.

There is so much uplifting musical content available everywhere; if you search for such content, you will find them. As you listen, you will discover that you are becoming a highly optimistic individual. Optimism is one of the crucial traits you need as you step forward; a happy person doesn't have it all, but he has faith in their future, and that is enough. A song that makes me optimistic is called "I Gotta Feeling" by The Black Eyed Peas. "Good Feeling" by my friend Flo Rida is another song that is sure to lift you up. In fact, it has become a sort of anthem for my movement to uplift military veterans around the world.

Music is Medicine

If you haven't been intentionally using music in your life, it is time to get started! Music is more than sounds that help us dance or feel good at a party.

Suppose you feel overwhelmed, anxious, and sad. In that case, you will not experience the bliss of transitioning from where you are to where you desire to be. But there is hope and help through music; start listening to music you like and music that uplifts your spirit. As you do, you will gain positive thoughts, clarity, and direction, empowering you to transition without fear and uncertainty.

As you spend time listening to music, learning something new every day would also be a good way to spend your time. Some people feel less inspired and frightened of transitions because of the "waiting period" that happens in between. They wonder, "What do I do while waiting?" Read the next chapter for some answers.

11

LEARN SOMETHING NEW EVERY DAY

A pregnant woman looks forward to the day she delivers her baby. But, for most parents, the nine-month waiting period is one with mixed emotions. They are excited at the start, and midway into it, parents obsessively plan for the baby's arrival. Then, in the final stages, they are anxious to have the birth over and done with.

Becoming a parent is also a transition, and the period of parental leave is quite essential. Likewise, a new graduate applying for a job in several organizations has a period of waiting until they finally hear back from the company and get the job they want. If someone is starting a business, they must wait until the business venture is fully operational.

So, within the transitional periods of our lives, there is a waiting phase, and the big question is, what do you do when you wait? If you are idle, doing nothing, you would be prone to depression and anxiety because you would always wonder, "What's next?"

While waiting, you should stay engaged, and this means aiming to learn something new daily. Even when you're not waiting for anything, you should still try to learn something new.

Learning something new will keep you occupied until you fully transition. And after you have successfully transitioned, this will help you remain productive.

That's an exciting word—*productive!*

Some think the waiting period is an unproductive stage. It's like going on a trip, or being on a long commute. Some people may wonder, "What do you do until you arrive at your destination?"

Well, you can read a book, learn a new language, develop a new hobby, use your hands to create something, watch an insightful documentary, chat with the person sitting next to you to make a new friend, or even watch as you pass through cities.

You must find ways of staying productive. Don't accept the idea that the in-between periods are unproductive and that you have to "wait" until something happens.

Your life has to remain whole while you transition to civilian life; you need to develop skills, learn new ideas, stay connected to impactful activities, and continue to thrive even as you make this transition.

Unfortunately, some veterans get back to civilian life and cannot reconcile their past and present. Hence, they lay around doing absolutely nothing! Soon enough, they feel like life has passed them by; they feel angry, sad, disappointed, and drained, and they ultimately give up. But imagine if the same veterans took charge of their lives by staying committed to learning something new. They would have something to look forward to every day.

Benefits of Learning Something New

It Reduces Stress

Learning something new or developing new hobbies are stress relievers. As you break free from your predictable routine, you give your brain something to think about other than the constant fears for the future. Every day, the things you do are not just temporary distractions; they are ideas and activities that help your mind think about things other than what causes you stress.

It Helps You Gain Confidence

All educational and insightful processes help someone gain and build confidence. This also applies to the things you learn daily. You will become very confident with your journey because you value yourself.

So, when you show up in the new phase of your life,

you enter it with a wealth of knowledge instead of apprehension. All you learn will become very useful to you as you go. This should be your goal.

It Gets You Ahead

Whatever you learn will add to your knowledge and help you get ahead in life. It will help you become more relatable, interesting, and fun.

Suppose you are a fresh graduate seeking a job. These new activities could help you stay active and converse and network better with others.

Whatever knowledge you gain as you transition will be a bonus, so it doesn't matter what you learn. Find any practical, fun, and educational activity.

It Improves Your Mental Health

Another reason why you should learn something daily is that it improves your mental health. You will feel energized, emotionally balanced, and excited because you have something to look forward to every day. Being idle has negative impacts on your mental well-being; you would feel drained without even doing anything. No wonder most people struggle to get out of bed.

Let's reverse that. Instead, you could try taking up new craft lessons where you use your hands to create something. This keeps your mind fresh and charged throughout the day.

If you have new and fun things to learn, you will feel that kick and excitement, making every day a unique opportunity to edge closer to your new life stage without emotionally draining transitions.

You Get to Have Fun

Learning something new is also important because you get to have fun! Always remember that if you enjoy the transitional phase, you won't struggle with it. So, aim for fun, and one of the best ways to do that is to learn something fun daily.

Remember the analogy we used about going on a trip? So, if you are on a long journey, what can you do to make it fun? First, of course, you want to have snacks, maybe a book, or a fun travel buddy. Now, you must do the same with your transition journey.

You would have fun doing something new and something that makes you happy. No one would worry about being anxious or worried about the transitional process if they were meaningfully engaged by doing fun things.

For example, have you ever done karaoke? What about swimming with dolphins? The point is you can have a lot of fun doing something new every day.

Set an Excellent Example

When you start learning new things again, you inspire them to take action. Look at how my life turned out. I didn't think I'd be in public office after getting out of the military. And now, through this book, I can inspire others to attain a resilient transition just as I have.

If you have kids, you want them to learn things that will allow them to thrive and adjust well when changes come into their lives. If children see you struggle in your transitions, that wouldn't be a very good example for them and that wouldn't help prepare them for their own transitions.

You can show your enthusiasm and teach them a life lesson when you use that period to learn something new.

Rediscover Yourself

When you dedicate yourself to learning every day, you start to rediscover yourself. However, sometimes people feel lost while transitioning. That feeling comes from leaving a comfortable and predictable lifestyle and moving into an uncertain future.

You need to know that transition could birth rediscovery, and you strengthen that process when you start learning new things. While learning new things, you will be amazed by the abilities that you will discover and you'll be empowered to step into your new phase without fear.

Develop the Right Attitude

First, you have to connect with your inner child because children like to experiment and enjoy figuring things out. But as adults, we tend to be dismissive toward learning new things, and we tend to believe that we already know everything. But, of course, that is not true!

We start to learn less when we stop being like kids, so if you want to learn something new daily, you need to connect with your inner child. Think of yourself as a child, what you wanted to do, and whether you can do those things now. Now is the time to find out what you want to do and explore the possibility of doing those things again.

Are you musically inclined? Do you want to read about something new, or are you passionate about one of your hobbies?

Connecting to your inner child also helps you become fearless. Nothing will hold you back from trying, even when you make mistakes.

Be Curious About Your Environment

There are so many things you could learn about or learn to do, but you won't know where to start if you ignore your environment. For example, some people learn how to garden, take care of their pets, or even simply drop their kids off at school.

These are just some things they can do that help them rebalance their lives. There is so much inspiration in your environment, but you will only see it if you pay attention. Starting with your environment also helps you start from familiar territory to the unfamiliar.

Home is an excellent place to start. Look around and find what you can learn. You can always build on those lessons. Where you live will be full of history. Perhaps your house was built hundreds of years ago. Who lived there then? What did the road you live on look like back then?

For me, it was interesting to come back to New York after being in the service for thirty years. I began to rediscover my home state by traveling to a new town every day. Additionally, I learned how to cook by using Google to find a new recipe every day. Then I got my new dog Private First Class Diesel from Chasin' Tail Rescue in North Carolina—that was a daily adventure that forced me to learn. These were the things that helped me turn a negative mindset into a very positive one.

Always Do Something You've Never Done Before

Irrespective of what you do, ensure you do something you've never done before—something new you can learn and add to your record. For example, suppose you are a recent graduate who mainly uses Microsoft Word for assignments. You could think about learning new things like Microsoft Excel or some other app or tool that would make you more competitive. Keep learning every day. Soon enough, every little bit will all add up.

Use the Internet

The internet has more than enough information on the kind of things you can learn daily. Maybe you've run out of ideas because you haven't intentionally searched the internet. You can find exciting, fun, and educational things you can do daily. The more you do new things and consistently search the internet, the more productive you become.

Engage in Fun Activities with a Friend

If you struggle with learning something new daily, try it with a friend. Of course, this idea depends on the kind of personality you have—quieter and more introverted people don't mind doing things themselves.

If you are more extroverted, get someone you can do something fun with like play tennis, go swimming, do yoga, or play a monopoly game. If you are a veteran and you have a fellow veteran friend, this would be an excellent time to engage in fun activities together.

Learning something new every day will always help you through the transition phase, so take this seriously.

You don't have to learn something massive daily. Sometimes it could be reading a book and learning something about history. The point is that you need to get busy and engaged so you are not caught up in a web of confusion and pressure about the next phase.

Improve Mental Health Through Energy-Healing Exercises

I have been practicing different energy-healing techniques and exercises for a couple of years. These very helpful practices were all classes offered at the Veterans Administration Hospital. I would highly recommend that every able veteran take these types of classes. I truly believe doing so will help drastically improve and heal you.

Energy healing is nothing but channeling the universal life force to correct energy imbalances in our system, which are the hidden cause of most of our diseases. We are energy beings, so all our ailments are rooted in energy imbalances. All physical or mental tension is an indication that there is a blockage in the energy flow in our bioenergetic system. Sometimes, merely clearing these blockages is enough, as the body's natural healing abilities take care of restoring the affected part back to health. I have tried yoga, Deepak Chopra meditation, tai chi, and reiki. I honestly believe that all of these can drastically change a person's mental health.

Yoga

Yoga can train us to focus our minds in more valuable ways. This keeps us from engaging our minds in ruminative thinking and in the creative things we do to soothe away our worries exacerbated by rumination. That keeps us from behaving in ways that get labeled as mental disorders. It is easiest to retrain your brain while doing something you enjoy. If you enjoy physical movement, then yoga is a great practice. I personally enjoy the teaching of yoga by Sadhguru from India.

Meditation

Meditation is an excellent and effective way to relieve mental stress, anxiety, uncontrolled thoughts, restlessness, insomnia, and other mental conditions. When a person's body is relaxed in the meditated state, they feel less stressed, tense, and their mind is at ease. The person recognizes that they are in control and gives them a chance to take a break during their busy day and rid themselves of certain stressors. Meditation diminishes evil thoughts and helps people heal from symptoms of stress and anxiety.

Tai Chi

Tai chi is a superb way to improve overall mood and mental stability. It's good for anxiety as it's a sort of meditative visualization while the body moves in slow, flowing, deliberate movements. Tai chi is for all ages, not just older people. It improves the joints and blood flow and lowers blood pressure.

Reiki

Reiki is a Japanese healing technique that improves what's called "life force energy" around the body. This subtle energy can become blocked by stress, possibly due to negative feelings such as fear, worry, doubt, anger, anxiety, and self-judgment.

The American Institute of Stress[1] estimates that 75% to 95% of all visits to doctors are related to stress, which can cause minor aches to major health concerns.

By promoting the removal of stress and tension from the body through deep relaxation, reiki can directly impact healing and health. Reiki treatment enhances relaxation, induces peace, and lessens stress. Reiki healing increases the supply of life force energy and aids in recovery by bringing the chakras, the different energy points in your body, into alignment and balance. With the physical, mental, and spiritual aspects in balance, the body's own healing mechanism starts functioning better.

I recommend doing any of the mentioned activities that you enjoy. If you enjoy it, you'll have an easier time making the time and effort to do it. If these energy-healing techniques don't please you, don't beat yourself up—there are plenty of other options to try to achieve the same outcome.

From staying engaged daily, we move on to learning the importance of healing yourself using the THREE ESSENTIALS: food, sleep, and exercise. So, as you transition to civilian life, treat yourself to a delicious meal, some nice rest, and maybe some cardio. Get all the details in the next chapter.

12

HEAL WITH FOOD, SLEEP, AND EXERCISE

W hen moving from one life phase to another, regardless of what happened in the previous phase, work on improving your overall wellness and get ready for the new phase. If you have experienced hardship while serving in the military, this transition time allows you to heal as you enter the civilian world.

When we say *healing*, we refer to wholesomeness, wellness, and stability due to being in a safe mental space. You may need to heal invisible wounds. For all kinds of healing, three essential pillars are crucial: food, sleep, and exercise.

We cannot be successful if we only focus on our resume or career plans; it is also essential that we take a holistic approach to heal from any sort of wound. If you are sick, unhealthy, and vulnerable to diseases when transitioning, you won't be able to maximize the opportunities in this new level.

So, in this chapter, you will learn the importance of these three crucial pillars and how to utilize them to transform your life. Let's start in the kitchen and talk about food!

Food

You need good nutrition to stay healthy and strong. Globally, there is increased awareness of the importance of eating better meals. But eating healthy doesn't mean you must go on a diet; it is not necessarily about losing weight. Instead, eating healthy and committing to wellness means feeling good about yourself both physically and mentally as you consume food.

Food can fuel and heal your body *if* you eat nutritious meals with all the right vitamins and minerals your body needs. You've got to eat balanced meals and be mindful of what you drink as well. Additionally, you must avoid eating processed meals, fried foods, and foods high in sugar or salt.

For your body to be empowered and sustain enough energy for the next stage, it needs more vitamins and minerals, which means you will need more fruits, vegetables, and lots of water, fats, proteins, whole grains, and other healthy foods. In addition, eating healthy helps you maintain good heart health as you are growing older. This approach will help protect you from cardiovascular and other diseases.

Healthy eating habits also enable you to develop

stronger bones and teeth now and in the future, thus preventing tooth decay and osteoporosis. Eating the right kind of food will put you in a better mood and raise your energy levels because "you are what you eat." If you eat unhealthy foods, you will often feel drained and susceptible to illnesses.

Healthy eating helps you feel better and more energized for your transitions; you will have more energy to take on your next phase if you are constantly eating well. Healthy eating also increases blood flow to your brain, thus reducing the risk of Alzheimer's disease.

Did you also know that making better food choices affects your psychological well-being? Choosing healthier foods can make you happier and more satisfied in life. In recent studies, researchers found that having a healthy diet can help you better absorb tryptophan.[1] This amino acid can be converted into serotonin (happy hormone) in the brain. This is why when people feel sad, experts recommend eating high-protein foods like turkey and salmon.

Researchers[2] have proven that people are more ready for change with a healthy diet and normal hormonal levels and are more likely to build emotional resilience, both of which are required if you want to transition smoothly from military to civilian life.

Listen to your body as you eat and stop eating foods that harm your body. If you frequently drink soda, you will feel bloated almost all the time. You will not only gain excessive weight but also increase your heart disease and cancer risk. If you drink water instead, you will experience weight loss rapidly, flush out toxins from your body, and boost your metabolic rate. So sometimes it's not just what you eat, it's also what you drink.

Now, here are some great food ideas you can incorporate into your meal plan:

- Fatty fish such as salmon are healthy and rich in Omega-3 fatty acids, reducing your risk of depression.
- Fermented food such as yogurt is an excellent addition to your meal plan because it contains probiotics that maintain a healthy gut. Other kinds of fermented food include kimchi and sauerkraut.
- Oats are also excellent (a good breakfast option), which you can enjoy in many ways. Oats are rich in fiber, which aids the digestion of carbs. It also stabilizes blood sugar levels.
- Nuts are also recommended, especially if you consume them fresh and daily. Nuts are rich in protein and healthy fats, making them the perfect superfood for your diet.
- Fruits are rich in vitamins, micronutrients, and minerals. If you want to indulge in something sweet, eat fruit.
- Eat a wide variety of vegetables. Start with

leafy greens and high-fiber root vegetables such as carrots. These vegetables are high in fiber, which could protect you from mood swings and depression: 2-3 cups of vegetables are all you need for your daily intake.

- Drink plenty of water: at least 8 glasses daily to stay hydrated and refreshed.

Whenever you feel blue or down, you may crave high-sugar foods such as cookies and ice cream to feel good. These foods can lift your spirits, but you will feel tired and drained after the sugar rush. Instead, you should aim for wholesome foods that can boost your overall health and start you on a positive routine.

Sleep

After enjoying a great meal filled with vitamins, minerals, and other nutrients, ensure that you get good sleep. Good sleep is vital for healing, but unfortunately, too many things interfere with our natural sleep cycles. During this transition phase, you may be dealing with anxiety, which causes you to feel like sleep is difficult to achieve.

However, despite everything we deal with, sleep time should be prioritized. Poor sleep patterns are strongly linked to weight gain,[3] affecting your metabolism. And if you are not sleeping at night, you're probably chewing on late-night snacks, eating more calories than required. But good sleepers eat fewer calories: a benefit they enjoy from being well rested.

Good sleep also improves concentration and productivity as it plays a vital role in brain function. You will experience better cognition, increased productivity, performance, and even increased concentration. If you sleep well, you are less likely to suffer from depression and anxiety.[4] Most people with mental health issues have poor sleep patterns.

Recent researchers have found a direct correlation between sleep quality and psychological well-being. This may be because sleep helps normalize our hormone levels.[5] An example is cortisol (stress hormone). With more cortisol, people are likely to feel frustrated and agitated, which leads to poor self-regulation and decision making.

Another hormone that sleep helps balance is estrogen. An imbalance of estrogen in the body can make anxiety less bearable and less manageable. But with correction through sleep, people are less vulnerable to triggers that may lead to anxiety.

Aside from these, sleep is crucial for improving your immune function[6] and repairing whatever has gone wrong in your body. Those who sleep less than 7 hours daily will get the common cold much faster than those who sleep for 8 hours or more.

So, if you often get colds, headaches, or feel feverish, it is time to check if you are getting the right amount of sleep. If you are not sleeping well enough, get up to 8 hours of sleep (consistently), and you will always feel rejuvenated.

Exercise

Good and healthy food, checked! Restful sleep, checked! So, what's next? Exercise! You've got to keep fit and maintain a consistent fitness regimen because it has multiple health benefits.[7] When you are active, you build yourself mentally and physically to create the perfect mindset and body for your transition.

Engaging in exercise also helps you feel happier because exercise boosts the production of your happy hormone. Have you ever spent time in the gym, and afterward, you felt calmer and more energized? Well, that's because exercise improves your mood while reducing anxiety, stress, and depression.

If you are going through a transition where you are still unsure about your next move, you may be tempted to live a sedentary lifestyle, and this would cause you to put on weight. Well, you need to get off that couch, get rid of the junk food, and start exercising because that is how you can get rid of bad fat and maintain a healthy weight.

Exercise helps you maintain stronger muscles and bones. Physical activities stimulate muscle building (especially weightlifting), particularly when you pair it with protein intake. If you are older, you need to take exercise seriously. Otherwise, you will lose muscle mass, muscle function, and increase your risk of injury. Exercise also reduces your risk of chronic pain. If you don't exercise frequently, you will be prone to chronic diseases because your blood isn't circulating properly. But regular exercise helps keep your blood circulating and your heart rate at an average level.

Contrarily, lack of exercise can cause a significant increase in belly fat, making you susceptible to type 2 diabetes, early death, and heart disease. Therefore, a daily routine is recommended.

Some people shy away from exercising because they don't want to lift heavy weights or spend long hours in the gym trying out various equipment. But the good news is, you don't have to start with all of that stuff. If you have not been exercising, you can start with easy and fun exercise routines such as taking long walks, jogging, swimming, using the treadmill, or even dancing.

At the beginner stage, your aim is to start building up strength. You can begin with minor activities that can keep you motivated and consistent. For example, walk around your neighborhood, take a walk around the beach, play football or any other sport you enjoy. This will help you remain physically fit. You will discover that healing is gradually taking place, and you feel energized even on days when you don't exercise.

Exercise is also great for healthy skin and protects you from oxidative stress, which happens when your body's antioxidant defenses fail at repairing the damages caused by free radicals to your cells. Through exercise, you can enjoy better sleep quality and relaxation. Exercise stimulates the recuperative process when you fall asleep afterward, and this helps you relax.

Have you engaged in some form of exercise today? If you haven't, it is not too late to get some activity in. So climb the stairs, ride a bike, walk around your neighborhood, and stay fit!

The process of attaining resilient transitions is a consistent and thorough one that cuts across varying facets. While focusing on what to do next, you also want to ensure that you are thriving mentally, physically, and emotionally.

To summarize, this chapter discussed the role and importance of food, sleep, and exercise in your transition. Remember, watch what you eat, be intentional about eating healthy meals, get the recommended amount of sleep daily to be mentally fit, and stay physically fit and active.

The following chapter will cover the most important law of the universe—the universal law of attraction. How can you leverage the power of the law of attraction to live life to the fullest? Let's find out in the next chapter!

13

THE UNIVERSAL LAW OF ATTRACTION

The universal law of attraction is one of the most powerful laws in the universe. Just like the law of gravity, it works irrespective of your faith in it or not. For example, if someone says, "I don't believe in the law of gravity," and jumps off a high-rise building, what do you think will happen to them? Of course, the individual is going to fall and hit the ground.

No one needs to believe in the law of gravity for it to work, and this is also true for the universal law of attraction. Just like gravity is always working around us, the universal law of attraction is also working. And you need to take advantage of it in your transition.

Did you know that you are always in a state of creation? Every second and minute you live on this earth is a creative moment: You create your future today with your thoughts. You are also creating consciously or subconsciously. You cannot take a break from it, and neither can you decide to not create because creation never ends.

Some people are skeptical about the law of attraction; they wonder whether it really works. But if you plant a seed in healthy soil, water it, and provide all it needs to grow, would you be shocked if it grew? You wouldn't be surprised because that is the natural order of things. The seed has to grow because it is planted in the right environment.

Now, your thoughts are like skin to the seed, and your life experiences, especially your future, are the fruit the seed produces. Wherever you are right now is a product of what you thought about in the past, so your life is not a coincidence.

The universal law of attraction makes it possible for us to have infinite possibilities, live in abundance, and enjoy an extraordinary life. With the law of attraction, you have the key to achieving lasting success, and it all begins with you using it intentionally.

When you wake up in the morning, what are the thoughts in your mind? What do you spend time thinking about the entire day? Are you in touch with your emotions? What kind of pictures are you creating in your mind? What kind of information about your next phase are you holding on to? Are you aware of the power of your thoughts?

These questions are crucial in helping you understand how universal laws work. Now, as someone in a transitional phase, you may feel apprehensive about your chances for success when you transition. You may be anxious because other people who have transitioned have failed, and you're constantly thinking that you would also fail.

Well, guess what? If you consistently hold on to those thoughts, you will fail. Yes, you will, because that is how the universal laws work, and it doesn't matter if you are not conscious about them. So, this chapter is a call for INTENTIONALITY and a reminder that you are constantly creating.

Even right now, you are creating your future. If you are intentional, you will create positive images to create the kind of future you want. Isn't it incredible that our imagination and thoughts give us our creative abilities? Whatever you want to achieve as you transition is possible, so start by thinking the right thoughts and tapping into the power of the universal law of attraction.

Consider a magnet and a metal object. These two are naturally attracted to each other and will naturally come together. You are the magnet, and the metal is what you are asking the universe to grant you. If you are constantly filled with positive thoughts, you will attract positivity from the universe.

Two Things to Note:

- If you send out positive energy to the universe by being appreciative and feeling happy, joyful, and passionate, you will attract the same energy in return.

- But if you always feel stressed out, drained, bored, bitter, angry, and resentful, you will send out negative energy and receive all of that in your life.

You are in the cockpit of this transitional phase, and it is up to you to determine the outcomes. Just like a pilot that flies an aircraft, you are the captain of your life and your future. So, stop with the complaints, pity parties, and blaming others. No one else is to blame but you, so it is time to wake up from your assumptions and take control of your life. When the pilot loses control, the plane crashes, and people die. Likewise, if you lose control, you will also crash. You might think that I'm being harsh, that I don't understand your particular situation. I do understand, and what I see is a strong, capable person who is resilient and can achieve every positive thing they desire. Negative self-talk will make you unproductive and self-destructive; I encourage you to have a positive mindset and use positive affirmations instead.

Even before I fully transitioned into civilian life, I envisioned what I wanted. I used the law of attraction to attract what I wanted. I wanted success, progress, stability, and prosperity in this new season of my life, and I got them. Oh, what a remarkable feeling it is to live the visions you have for your life! I want you to experience this level of freedom and oneness with the universe, and the steps below will help you.

How to Use the Law of Attraction

When you understand the law of attraction and how it works, you will consciously and intentionally build the kind of life you want. Then, it is possible to choose how to respond differently to the different phases of your life. It is possible to focus and concentrate on what you want in life because you know you will get it. And it is also possible to deliberately choose the kind of experiences you want by concentrating on what makes you feel good.

First Step: ASK

First, you've got to ask the universe for what you want. Don't ask for what you don't wish to have, and don't assume that the universe knows what you like or don't like.

You send out daily requests to the universe and your subconscious mind through thoughts, so thinking is the first way to ask. Think about what you want, read about the things you want, and give attention to these ideas.

Some people give attention to irrelevant and random ideas. In other words, they live life by default and don't bother controlling their thoughts. If you have been doing this, you need to become more intentional about asking through your thoughts.

The universal law of attraction requires you to ASK! You have to THINK it and then SAY it! Be sure of what you want and ask for them, and the universe will bring those things your way.

Perhaps you want this new phase to be full of laughter. Or maybe you want a sense of purpose. Start making requests and believe in them. You can ask through affirmations, prayers, and even through visualization.

Sometimes people feel so intimidated by the entire process that they ask for significantly smaller things. They do that because they fear that they are asking for "too much." But what is too much? There is no such thing as too much when it comes to what you want, so ask, pray, and speak about what you want; the universe is listening and will make it happen.

When thinking about asking the universe for anything, remember that it is akin to getting a blank check from a billionaire who wants to give you whatever you want. What do you do with a blank check? You write what you want, and you will get it.

Second Step: BELIEVE

After asking, you have to be open to receiving by first believing. How can you be rewarded if you don't believe? The believing part is often the most challenging, so some people want to skip it. Be consistent and continue to make your goals known and manifest your reality by speaking it into existence.

The receiving process entails building and maintaining a positive, expectant mindset as you go through your day, knowing that something good is about to happen to you. When you step out of your house, and someone does something nice for you, you are not taken aback. You get excited about that experience because you have asked for kindness and believed that it would happen.

Some people have limiting beliefs that prevent them from allowing the thoughts of abundance and happiness to flow in their lives. If you have such limiting beliefs, which may include thinking you are not worthy of good things, not believing that you are strong enough, it is time to make changes. It is time to let those limiting beliefs go. After asking, you need to believe and trust the universe. Believe that everything you've asked will come to you, and don't bother about the how or who will make it happen. Your role here is to believe and hold on to your belief until it happens.

Now, sometimes we get a bit impatient when things don't happen immediately. But the universal law of attraction is not magic. It is not a magic wand you wave in the air to get what you need. Be patient with the process, keep believing, and trust in the power of the request you've made to the universe. Over time, it will all align with your future realities.

Third Step: RECEIVE

Lastly, you've got to receive what you've asked for and believed you would get. You must become a vibrational match for what you've asked for and wanted to attract. You can become a vibrational match by focusing on positive emotions of appreciation, love, joy, and gratitude every day.

Use your thoughts to draw your requests close to you, and soon enough, you will start to see these thoughts manifest in your life in real time. Of course, the fact that you are doing this doesn't mean you wouldn't have an occasional negative thought. But when those negative thoughts creep into your mind, instantly replace the ideas with a positive and empowering thought.

It takes time to switch from negative to positive thoughts. However, the more you do it consciously, the easier it becomes. You can get all the miracles you desire in a positively enabled mental space. Start today with intentional thoughts and you will enjoy tremendous gifts from the universe.

If you need money for the transition to become successful, use the universal law of attraction to make it happen. You can establish financial abundance in your life by focusing on prosperity and money flowing into your life. Think about the checks and bank credit notifications coming into your life. Write yourself a check for the sum of money you wish to manifest.

Place the check at a visible location and every time you look at it, believe that you can get it. Be thankful for all you possess, no matter how little. Don't wait until you have all the money you need before expressing gratitude; moments of gratitude create a vibrational match for your future financial abundance.

The same principles apply to everything else: love, career, relationships, guidance, increase, and peace. Whatever you need for your future, you can get it, so remember the three steps: Ask, believe, and receive, and the universe will align for your advantage.

The next chapter is the final one, and it talks about how your possibilities are limitless. Armed with the knowledge of the universal law of attraction, you can do anything! Are you ready to learn how to recognize that your opportunities are limitless?

Great! Let's go!

14

ENJOY YOUR LIMITLESS POSSIBILITIES

I am thrilled at all the things you will achieve as you experience resilient transitions from one phase of your life to another. As we come to the end of this book, it is essential that you understand that your possibilities are limitless. There is no limit on the results you can get and what you can achieve.

Why Is Mindset So Important?

Well, here's the thing. If you don't believe that your possibilities are limitless, you will feel as if something or someone is holding you back in this new chapter of your life. You will feel unprepared and lack confidence, which is a recipe for disaster. So I want you to understand why mindset is crucial.

When transitioning from one significant life experience to another, these questions may pop into your mind:

"Am I ready for this new phase?"
"Do I have the tools to thrive in this new season?"
"What if I fail?"
"What if my contemporaries do better than me?"

Sometimes, these questions signal that the person is anxious and unsure about the future. In that state of uncertainty, they would give off the wrong energy to the universe and mess up the opportunities that come their way.

Now, it is OK to feel uncertain about your next move (we all have the jitters), but it is not OK to allow those feelings to fester for a long time. You need to protect your energy and maintain a keen focus on your goals because that is how you will thrive.

I want to particularly encourage veterans who develop cold feet when transitioning into civilian life. Yes, it can be mentally and physically tasking. But you need to believe that your possibilities and the things you can achieve are endless, regardless of your age.

Look at me! At my age, some people would think I should retire somewhere and just sit on my recliner, but here I am, still taking on a political career. So much more lies ahead of you, but you need to have unwavering faith in your abilities.

Life itself is full of possibilities, and this is why we hear and read stories of greatness—men and women who had fallen many times and suddenly found their rhythm. But the struggles we face often make it hard for us to see the prize ahead. Yet, there is a prize ahead, and you've got to look beyond your current discomfort to see it.

A pregnant woman must deal with many uncomfortable experiences. She has to deal with constant backaches, fatigue, nausea, pains all over her body, and even difficulty moving as the pregnancy advances. However, she doesn't suddenly get rid of the baby at six months because she wants some relief. What keeps her going? It's the thought of holding her baby in her arms, and that end goal is what she holds on to when she feels nauseous in the morning.

Now, what is your end goal? What do you want to achieve with this next phase of your life, and do you believe you can get it?

When you are about to transition, it might seem like everything is coming at you simultaneously. You could get overwhelmed and feel like you need to make quick decisions. I want you to know that the "difficult" phase, is but for a moment. You will never truly discover your potential if you make those difficult times the focus of your life.

You have been equipped with so much information and practical steps from this book for you to have a resilient transition. You are ready. But for you to feel prepared, you must believe in yourself and in your ability to thrive wherever planted.

Have you ever seen a cactus plant in a desert? Have you ever wondered why and how the cacti survive in such arid areas? There is a lesson on embracing endless possibilities through observing the cactus plant. The plant has no leaves; there is most likely no rain in the desert or anyone to water the plant. But the cactus doesn't die.

Instead, it stores water in its thick stems and has a protective covering that keeps the stored water inside. Some cactus species can live for two years without getting additional water. Under the sun and in the driest conditions, the cactus thrives because it relies on the water it has inside.

Now, what do you have inside? Do you have fear, or faith and confidence that you will make it?

What you have inside ultimately determines if you will harness your limitless possibilities. So, it is essential that, like the cactus, you retain the goodness within you as you navigate the initial transition period.

How to Harness Your Limitless Possibilities

Be a Risk-Taker

You've got to take CALCULATED risks! These are risks you have accessed and concluded are worth taking.

Sometimes when transitioning, we are looking for a safe compass. But it would be best if you didn't wait for that safe compass all the time; it's okay to take a different approach to see what lies ahead.

There are authors who had written multiple books before one finally became a bestseller or award winner. There are musicians who had released numerous songs before finally making a hit record. If they had stopped taking risks and creating, they probably wouldn't have reached success.

Continue to try new ideas and take calculated risks and you, too, will find success.

Get Out of the Comfort Zone

You cannot harness your limitless possibilities and rise above your current level if you don't get out of your comfort zone. Your comfort zone prevents you from making extra effort to be great.

For example, you learned to write blog posts and mastered that. You shouldn't stop there. Don't get stuck with just that skill and remain where it's comfortable.

The point is that you cannot grow in a comfortable place! Get out of your comfort zone and keep trying new things, exposing yourself to new ideas, and exploring new terrains. The more you explore, the more you will push the envelope and broaden your mindset on what you can achieve.

Fail Forward

Failure is part of what you should expect on this journey, but here is what you can do with it: Fail forward! Failing forward means being persistent instead of accepting failure and giving up.

For example, you will have many activities and career choices after your military service. Sometimes you may have a perfect start to your career of choice, but as you try to fit in, you may find yourself failing. Instead of feeling bad about it, go look back and try to figure out *why* you failed, and then try again.

Think of a toddler who is just starting to learn how to walk. The child falls multiple times and picks himself up each time to try again. That's how we all learned how to walk and look at ourselves today! Some people even win gold medals for how fast they run.

That child failed forward; he didn't fall and then sat down—he kept going, and today, he is like you and me, walking tall and thriving.

Build Yourself Strong in Tough Seasons

While on this transition path, you will face very tough times, and I am saying this to prepare you so it won't get the best of you.

If you are keen on unleashing your limitless potential, you need to build yourself strong in those challenging times. Build mental, physical, and emotional strength because you will need it when entering the new stage.

You may get many rejections, a lot of nos, and face some stumbling blocks. However, if you remain focused and build resilience, you will have a resilient transition.

Trust Your Instincts

Sometimes the answer to the transition puzzle lies within us, but the question is, "Do you trust your instincts?" For example, if you are keen on starting a new business you feel passionate about, you will have initial conflicting thoughts.

But despite those, you will feel the urge to keep going, especially if you are passionate about it. That urge, kick, voice, or nudge is your instinct telling you that you can advance. If you don't go forward when your instincts urge you to, you may miss out on doing something great. So, trust your inner voice and stick with your intuition.

Fear is a Useful Motivational Tool

When you are getting close to your transition, you may begin to feel frightened about the next stage of your life. That is a natural response to uncertainty. We also must understand that fear is an emotional reaction to something that appears to be dangerous. Some people fear failure because it may cause them embarrassment. Fear is a powerful motivator because it makes us uncomfortable, and we want to move away from that discomfort toward our comfort zone. While it is powerful, the problem with fear motivation is that it can become stressful over time.

Now use that fear you feel as a tool to stay motivated throughout the process of transition. We can use fear as a ladder to get to our desired destination, and that is why you hear people say, "I did it, afraid." They leaped and acted on their goals while being afraid, and you can do the same. If you can conquer fear, you can unleash your ability to maximize limitless possibilities.

There are so many potential moments in this new and exciting chapter that can turn your life around in an instant, and who knows, it just might be during this transition you are about to make.

I often wonder what Elvis Presley, Jimi Hendrix, Ice-T, Morgan Freeman, and others who have transitioned from the military to civilian life were thinking as they left the service. They went on to become big celebrities after their transition.

I wonder what my dad, Dr. E.C. Foster, the first Black city council president in Jackson, Mississippi, was thinking when he was Specialist Foster transitioning from Keller Army Hospital in West Point, New York, to return to college life back at Jackson State University in the early 1960s.

Like those iconic figures, you have so many possibilities ahead of you that there are no limits to who you can become in your next chapter. Don't waste your time and energy whining about what has gone wrong with your life, or how things used to be while you were in your former situation.

Think about all the possibilities you can unlock now. Think like the cactus in the desert, and from deep within, believe in yourself. You can accomplish ANYTHING.

Live a FULFILLED life right now. Starting today, seek out what makes you happy and push yourself to accomplish your dreams. Surround yourself with the right people, express gratitude, move with confidence, and take calculated risks.

With this book, I am confident that you are on your way toward attaining a resilient transition. I am cheering you on as you prepare to take those big steps. Now let's finish off this entire process with my concluding recommendations that would propel you to take action.

CONCLUSION

When a significant change occurs in your life, it causes a shift in your perceptions that affects your entire life. Such turbulence makes us unsure about what to do next, and the uncertainty leaves us in an uncomfortable state of confusion. Regardless if we are transitioning into a role as a new mom, a civilian veteran, a new student, or a fresh graduate, it is never easy to transition and it puts us at risk for mental health issues.

However, regardless of the challenges we encounter in the transition, we can and we must develop a resilient mindset. A resilient mindset will enable you to go through the process and settle into your new reality with ease.

I started writing this book because I wanted to share my experiences and inspire you with real lessons learned that will enable you to develop resilience. I used to think that the Army was my whole life. But now I realize that, in addition to my military story, I have a post-military story, which keeps getting better every day.

In this book, I offer you a variety of options and ways through which you can attain a resilient transition: from the power of using music to manage stress, to being conscious of the vibrational energy that you emit to the world, the benefits of learning new things, and the incredible use of the universal law of attraction to manifest your desires. We have learned so much together, and at this stage, I'm confident you are mentally prepared to take on whatever challenges come your way.

Now, most people are wired to believe that when we get to the conclusion of a book, it signals the end of the learning process. Readers finish a book, and as soon as they close it, they instantly forget about all they've learned. Yes, the conclusion marks the end of your reading experience for now, but it is the START of your implementation process.

You've got to implement all you've learned because that is the only way you can truly attain a resilient transition. Think of a garden, a beautiful garden with thriving flowers. How do you think the gardener achieved such a feat? He had to till the soil, get the proper nutrients into the ground, plant the seeds, nurture the young plants, and take care of the plant as it grew.

Imagine someone else who also planned to plant a garden, gathered the seeds, fertilizer, and other necessary materials, then walked away. When that individual comes back in two years, there will be no garden. This shows us that it is not enough to KNOW how something works. While reading and learning are essential, implementation is key to success!

There is a saying: "Knowledge is power." But the question is, what do you do with the knowledge you gain? What happens next after gaining knowledge? Now that you know how to attain a resilient transition, what do you do with that knowledge?

The reality of times shows that it doesn't end with attaining knowledge; instead, it is the EXECUTION of knowledge that counts. You've got to become intentional with using what you've learned. Leverage this advantage with consistent application.

Execution helped me to finally gain the capacity to begin writing and ultimately finish this book. I feel a sense of relief, freedom, and resilience for being vulnerable enough to tell my truth. I am happy with myself for lifting the veil of a sanitized and guarded persona of perfection, transforming my story into the raw, uncomfortable, maybe unpopular downright truth. If this book inspires even one person to make a positive change in their life, it would have been well worth the effort that I've put into it.

I was intentional with asking the universe to make

me a published author in 2021. I then prepared myself by studying the subject matter, and I ultimately took action to execute my plan. As we come to the end of these heartfelt words on these important, life-changing pages, I encourage you to write down, review, and reflect on all we have unraveled and learned. Start implementing these today.

Refuse to feel down about your current state and use the tools you've gained to make resilient transitions. The difference between where you are and your next phase is execution. If you don't execute the strategies you've read, you will know so much but have very little results to show.

I have just two very important questions for you: How will you implement the teachings from this book into your daily life? How will you also share your incredible story of resilient transition with others who need your help? The answer lies in **intentional execution.**

Your possibilities are truly endless, and I believe that you are on the path toward maximizing all of life's opportunities. Your life is about to change because you are not supposed to be static. And when you encounter changes or challenges with each new phase, remember this book. Use the ideas gained to transform those challenges into a blissful new chapter of your amazing life.

Remember, there are many things that you can do to make any transition a breeze. There are plenty of resources and help out there. You are not alone. Believe in yourself. Look at the positive side of everything. Keep positive people in your circle, and trust that all will go right in your life starting now.

Repeat after me: What you believe, you will achieve.

Enjoy the journey of a wonderful life and expect the best out of yourself. You possess the information you need for any type of transition to not only be painless and easy but exciting and even fun.

There is a special gift for you in the next and final section: your first step toward implementation. Enjoy, and don't forget to execute everything that you've learned. Keep me posted on your progress. HOOAH!

MY SPECIAL GIFT TO YOU!

30 Days of Positive Affirmations

To help you implement all you've learned, I have put together a special gift that will help you through this transition phase. Your words matter! The words you speak to yourself matter. You must say what you want to see into existence.

Speak these affirmations consistently so that they become a permanent fixture in your subconscious mind. When I felt the weight of moving from military to civilian life, affirmations were quite helpful to me. I believe they will help you also.

Here are 30 days of positive affirmations you can use to reshape your experience and strengthen yourself through this phase of your life. Please note that the claims are universal and can be used for a wide array of issues.

Day 1
I love and accept myself.

I am in love with myself, and I accept myself. Today I love the person I am becoming, and I accept my life experiences as lessons that keep me focused. I accept my body and all positive thoughts, and I love my journey through life.

Day 2
I have clarity of purpose and strength in my heart.

I am a person of clarity and purpose with power in my heart. I know what to do and do it well, I excel in all things, and I am enabled for great exploits.

Day 3
I find fulfillment in all I do..

Today I find joy and fulfillment in all I do. The satisfaction I gain from today's work fuels my excitement to meet tomorrow's expectations. I am hopeful, strong, and satisfied with my efforts as they yield great results.

Day 4
I walk into a flourishing future.

My past experiences no longer hinder my current expectations nor my future projections. I have a flourishing future, and I walk into it with joy, excitement, and an unstoppable mindset.

Day 5
My potential for success is infinite.

I have an infinite potential for success, so today, I heap success upon success. I am on an onward and upward journey, and every day I unleash such possibilities through the projects I undertake.

Day 6
My efforts yield results.

All my efforts will yield substantial and long-term results, and there are no delays in my life. I embrace increase and growth today, I am optimistic, and if I don't get it, it won't stop me from trying again.

Day 7
My thoughts align with my actions.

I always think positive thoughts, and those thoughts align with my actions. When I think of empowering beliefs, I feel empowered to take action, which I manifest today.

Day 8
I have mastery over my feelings and emotions.

Emotions and feelings do not easily sway me as I have gained mastery over my feelings. I choose to be happy, hungry for success, and satisfied with my trajectory. I do not succumb to just any emotion; I feel and express only the emotion I choose.

Day 9
I am deserving of all the beautiful things that come my way.

I deserve all the beautiful things that happen to me, and I am conscious of more blessings coming my way. Today, good things happen to me as I step out to tackle new opportunities.

Day 10
I am in charge of my feelings, and I choose happiness.

I am conscious and in control of my emotions, so I choose joy. I will not be sad today; I will be happy, full of hope, and excited about my future as I surpass my goals.

Day 11
I am bold with life.

I am bold and courageous with life; therefore, I show up ready like a lion to overcome problems today. No fear will bring me down today, and whenever fear comes, I am bold enough to kick it out of my mind. My boldness always makes way for me.

Day 12
I prioritize myself and my growth.

Today, I prioritize my growth, I put myself first, and I am committed to my development. I am better than yesterday, and I am beyond successful because I have my priorities right.

Day 13
I have a resilient mindset.

My mindset is resilient and strong enough to continue even when I face tough challenges. I am resilient and persistent. I am the best at what I do, and I don't give up. I press on every day to win, and I do so joyfully!

Day 14
I see challenges as opportunities.

The challenges I face today are my opportunities to thrive. I am excited about challenges—I see them next door to possibilities—and I confidently take them down. Every challenge on my way today will pave the way for success, and I am mentally ready to take them all on.

Day 15
I am patient with my process.

Today I believe that good things take time. Therefore, I am patient with my process. It doesn't matter how long it will take; I will remain tenacious and patient until I achieve and surpass my goals.

Day 16
I am limitless and abounding with potential.

I have unlimited and abounding potential that makes me thrive. All I need to win with any venture is within me, and I tap into that reservoir of ideas to make progress.

Day 17
I am where I'm meant to be.

I am right now where I need to be, and I will make the most of this phase's opportunities. I am at the right place and timing for my life; this is the day for me to rise above and get one step closer to my ultimate goal.

Day 18
I am kinder to myself.

Today I am kinder to myself. I am kind with my words, thoughts, and actions such that my world is ruled by kindness. I do not say harsh words to myself today, even when under intense pressure, and I extend that kindness to others.

Day 19
My subconscious mind vibrates to a higher frequency.

My subconscious mind awakens and vibrates to a higher frequency beyond what I feel today. I envision myself at the highest level in this new stage and work toward attaining it without fear or anxiety.

Day 20
I free myself from the fears of the past.

Today I am free from past fears; there is no regret in my life, and my journey in the future is one free from my frightful past. I am inspired to rise above past failures and approach the future with a certainty of purpose.

Day 21
I don't compete with anyone else.

I appreciate other people who have made more progress than me while transitioning, but I do not compete with them. I am conscious of my journey, appreciative of my gifts, and refuse to compete with anyone else. Whenever I feel like competing, I am reminded of my journey.

Day 22
I live in good health.

I do not fall sick today; I am physically, mentally, financially, and emotionally healthy. Sickness has no control over my body; my healthy body stays strong, and I can do whatever I want to achieve today.

Day 23
I am blessed.

I am blessed today. Everywhere I go, I am blessed. I am a blessing to those in my world, and I am blessed with amazing people who love me. I am blessed with opportunities that open doors for me, and I am blessed with a tenacious spirit to pursue those opportunities.

Day 24
I am free from the pressure of impressing others.

I do not owe anyone a progress report today. I will pat myself on my back for doing well without focusing on the pressures from societal standards. My focus is on my goals, and I smash all of them today.

Day 25
I am not throwing a pity party today.

I will no longer throw pity parties and seek sympathy from others. I am powerful enough for this transition, and I will have great results irrespective of what I encounter today. NO PITY PARTIES!

Day 26
I am relaxed and stress-free.

Today, I am relaxed, happy, restful, and at peace with myself. I refuse to be stressed, and nothing can shake me even as I navigate this new experience. Whatever will cause me stress does not come my way today, and I thrive with whatever I do.

Day 27
I am more than an individual; I am powerful.

I am thankful for the power I embody as an individual. I am strong enough today to rise above challenges, and I withstand the pressures of the transition phase. I do not rely on my physical strength alone, and through my mental capacity, I find answers and solutions.

Day 28
I attract all I need.

Right now, I attract all I see in my mind and all I need to remain productive and successful. I attract goodwill, wealth, great thoughts, increased abilities, and self-love. Everything I need to be a better (mention what you are now) comes to me today and always.

Day 29
I overflow with positive emotions today.

Today, I overflow with an abundance of positive emotions as I go about my day. There is no sadness, depression, or pain in my day, and I am optimistic about my future even in this new stage of my life.

Day 30
I will thrive in this new phase.

I declare that in this new phase as a (civilian, new mom, new employee, graduate, etc.), I will win every day. Today opens the wells of possibility and progress for me, and I will conquer this new phase.

If this is your first time using affirmations, you might struggle at the start with remembering to say the words. So here are some helpful tips:

- Set reminders on your mobile phone, as this will help you take it seriously, and even if you have a hectic day, you will get it done.
- Print the affirmations and place them in a spot where you can see them and say them quickly. Put it on your fridge door, bathroom mirror, or by your bedside lamp.
- Enjoy and envision the words so that they become a part of you. SEE what you SAY, and soon enough, it will become your reality.

My Music Playlist for You

Music elevates your mood, and whenever you feel distressed, you can turn to music to feel better. It is an emotional support system that could swiftly transport you into a positive state.

So, along with words of affirmation, I would like to share my music playlist with you, which has immensely helped me transition, and I am sure it will help you.

These 30 songs have been found to be the most relaxing songs, according to a 2019 UK study by Smooth Radio and Rescue Remedy.[1] You can listen to them if you are looking to relax, fight anxiety, or just wanting to have a bit of quiet alone time.

A Spotify playlist is available for you at https://bit.ly/resilienttransition.

1. Louis Armstrong, "What a Wonderful World"
2. The Beatles, "Let It Be"
3. Elton John, "Your Song"
4. Adele, "Someone Like You"
5. Adele, "Hello"
6. Coldplay, "Fix You"
7. Aretha Franklin, "I Say a Little Prayer"
8. Enya, "Orinoco Flow"
9. Cat Stevens, "Morning Has Broken"
10. U2, "Beautiful Day"
11. Dido, "White Flag"
12. Keane, "Somewhere Only We Know"
13. Ed Sheeran, "Thinking Out Loud"
14. Bob Dylan, "Lay Lady Lay"
15. Eagles, "Peaceful Easy Feeling"
16. Norah Jones, "Come Away with Me"
17. Bobby McFerrin, "Don't Worry Be Happy"
18. Coldplay, "The Scientist"
19. Simon and Garfunkel, "America"
20. Thè Jackson 5, "I'll Be There"
21. David Gray, "Babylon"
22. Maroon 5, "She Will Be Loved"
23. Sam Smith, "Lay Me Down"

24. Katie Melua, "Nine Million Bicycles"
25. Ed Sheeran, "The A Team"
26. All Saints, "Pure Shores"
27. Lily Allen, "Smile"
28. Norah Jones, "Don't Know Why"
29. Corrine Bailey Rae, "Put Your Records On"
30. Lana Del Rey, "Summertime Sadness"

I would also like to share with you the music of a talented artist I had the pleasure of meeting recently at a park in Providence, Rhode Island. I was on a road trip one weekend and stopped for a rest break on my way back to New York and was pleasantly surprised by music that sounded magical. I left the park totally relaxed, energized, and motivated.

The artist is Yacouba Diabate from Burkina Fasso, West Africa. He is a master kora player, an instrument similar to the harp. His album entitled *Burkina* is a wonderful compilation of stress-relieving world music. The brilliant sounds of the kora bring happiness and tranquility, making it a perfect track for deep meditation. Learn more about him and his music at http://www.yacoubadiabate.com.

RESOURCES FOR VETERANS

Canada

Veteran Affairs Canada

Email: information@veterans.gc.ca

Telephone: +1-866-522-2122

TDD/TTY: 1-833-921-0071

Army, Navy, and Air Force Veterans in Canada

Email: anavets@storm.ca

Telephone: +1 416-259-4145

Korea

Korean War Veterans Association

KWVA National President: Jeffrey J. Brodeur:

kvamane@aol.com

KWVA National Secretary: Harold Trieber

Email: HaroldSki302@aol.com

Telephone: (217) 345-4414

Korea Defense Veterans Association
Email: contact@kdva.vet

Pakistan
Army Welfare Trust aka Askari Group of Companies
Email: infoawt@awt.com.pk
Telephone: +92-51-9272400-4
Fauji Foundation
Email: info@fauji.org.pk
Telephone: +92-51-595-1821

India
Indian Army Veterans Portal
Email: armyveteranscell@gmail.com
Email: rnwcorpus@gmail.com
Email: veteranscell-army@nic.in
Telephone: 011-2567-4762

Department of Ex-Servicemen Welfare
Dr. Pudi Hari Prasad - Joint Secretary (ESW)
Email: jsesw@nic.in
Telephone: 23011804
Maj Gen MK Sagoch - DG Resettlement
Email: dgr@desw.gov.in
Telephone: 26192351

United States of America
Department of Veterans Affairs (VA)
Website: http://www.va.gov

Contact: https://iris.custhelp.va.gov/
Local Offices:
https://www.va.gov/directory/guide/home.asp

Main Address:
810 Vermont Ave., NW
Washington, DC 20420

Toll-Free: 1-800-827-1000
TTY: 1-800-829-4833

Forms: http://www.va.gov/forms
Parent Agency: White House

LIST OF SOURCES

1. First Steps

1. Mayo Clinic. "Post-Traumatic Stress Disorder (PTSD)." July 6, 2018. https://www.mayoclinic.org/diseases-conditions/post-traumatic-stress-disorder/symptoms-causes/syc-20355967.
2. Mayo Clinic. "Depression." February 3, 2018. https://www.mayoclinic.org/diseases-conditions/depression/symptoms-causes/syc-20356007.
3. Mental Health Foundation. "Armed Forces and Mental Health." Accessed July 7, 2021. https://www.mentalhealth.org.uk/a-to-z/a/armed-forces-and-mental-health.
4. Shane, Leo III. "Suicide Remains Growing Concern for Younger Veterans, Survey Shows." *Military Times*, March 4, 2020. https://www.militarytimes.com/news/pentagon-congress/2020/03/04/suicide-remains-growing-challenge-for-younger-veterans-survey-shows/.
5. Cherry, Kendra. "How Listening to Music Can Have Psychological Benefits." VeryWellMind. December 10, 2019. https://www.verywellmind.com/surprising-psychological-benefits-of-music-4126866.
6. Schaefer, Hans-Eckhardt. "Music-Evoked Emotions—Current Studies." *Frontiers in Neuroscience* 11, no. 600 (2017). https://doi.org/10.3389/fnins.2017.00600.
7. Florida International University. "Project TREBLE." Accessed August 8, 2021. https://cbri.fiu.edu/all-research/project-treble/.
8. Novotney, Amy. "Music as Medicine." *Monitor on Psychology* 44, no. 10 (November 2013): 46. https://www.apa.org/monitor/2013/11/music.

2. My International Worldview

1. National Health Service. "Veterans: Priority NHS Treatment." June 13, 2018. https://www.nhs.uk/nhs-services/armed-forces-and-veterans-healthcare/veterans-priority-nhs-treatment/.
2. US Department of Veterans Affairs. "VA Home Page." Accessed August 8, 2021. https://www.va.gov/.
3. Stasha, Smiljanic. "How Many Veterans Are Homeless in the US 2021?" Last modified March 23, 2021. https://policyadvice.net/insurance/insights/homeless-veterans-statistics/.
4. Wilding, Mark. "The Challenges of Measuring Homelessness among Armed Forces Veterans: Service Provider Experiences in England." *European Journal of Homelessness* 14, no. 1 (2021). https://www.feantsaresearch.org/public/user/Observatory/2020/EJH/EJH_14_1-RN3-Web%5B1%5D.pdf.
5. Royal British Legion. "Literature Review: UK Veterans and Homelessness." Accessed August 8, 2021. https://www.britishlegion.org.uk/docs/default-source/campaigns-policy-and-research/litrev_uk_vets_homelessness.pdf?sfvrsn=110aad9f_2.
6. Veterans Affairs Canada. "VAC Home Page." Updated July 30, 2021. https://www.veterans.gc.ca/eng.
7. Kim, Gene, and Will Wei. "South Korea Requires All Males to Serve in the Military—Here's What It's Like." Insider. May 21, 2017. https://www.businessinsider.com/what-its-like-south-korea-mandatory-military-service-2017-5.

3. Suicide Prevention

1. Stop Soldier Suicide. "Veteran Suicides: Priority NHS Treatment." Accessed July 9, 2021. https://stopsoldiersuicide.org/vet-stats.
2. Richman, Mike. "Study: Veterans with Multiple Brain Injuries Twice as Likely to Consider Suicide, Compared with Those with One or None." US Department of Veteran Affairs. Accessed July 9, 2021. https://www.research.va.gov/currents/1118-Veterans-with-multiple-brain-injuries-twice-as-likely-to-consider-suicide.cfm.

3. Center for Deployment Psychology. "Suicide in the Military." Uniformed Services University of the Health Sciences. Accessed August 4, 2021. https://deploymentpsych.org/disorders/suicide-main.

4. Learning Resilience from Celebrities

1. Yagoda, Maria. "Stars Who Have Spoken Out about Their Struggles with Mental Health Issues." *People*, updated March 4, 2021, https://people.com/health/stars-who-have-mental-illnesses-mental-health-issues/.
2. Osaka, Naomi. "Naomi Osaka: 'It's O.K. Not to Be O.K.'" *Time,* July 8, 2021, https://time.com/6077128/naomi-osaka-essay-tokyo-olympics/.
3. Vantage Point Recovery. "Why Do Celebrities Experience Depression?" Accessed August 4, 2021. https://vantagepointrecovery.com/celebrities-experience-depression/.
4. MacMillan, Amanda. "20 Celebrities Who Battled Depression." Health. Updated April 23, 2013. https://www.health.com/condition/depression/20-celebrities-who-battled-depression.
5. Callahan, Chrissy. "Goldie Hawn Opens Up about Being 'Very Depressed' in Her 20s." Today. May 12, 2021. https://www.today.com/health/goldie-hawn-opens-about-depression-her-20s-t218143.
6. Mckenzie, Joi-Marie. "Oprah Winfrey Opens Up about Her Battle with Depression: 'I Was Behind a Veil.'" ABCNews. August 14, 2017. https://abcnews.go.com/Entertainment/oprah-winfrey-opens-battle-depression-veil/story?id=49206090.
7. Calhoun, Amanda J., and Jessica A. Gold. "'I Feel Like I Know Them': The Positive Effect of Celebrity Self-Disclosure of Mental Illness." *Academic Psychiatry* 44 (2020): 237–241. https://doi.org/10.1007/s40596-020-01200-5.
8. Douze, Kalila. "A Psychologist's Take on Mental Health for Musicians." Spotify for Artists. October 4, 2019. https://artists.spotify.com/blog/a-psychologists-take-on-mental-health-for-musicians.
9. NAMI Kenosha County. "300 Famous Individuals with Mental Health Issues, Illnesses, and Disorders." Accessed August 5, 2021.

https://www.namikenosha.org/famous-people-with-mental-issues.html.

10. Aiken, Chris. "What Leonard Cohen Can Teach Us about Depression." *Psychiatric Times,* May 28, 2020, https://www.psychiatrictimes.com/view/what-leonard-cohen-can-teach-us-about-depression.

11. Robinson, Jennifer. "John Denver: Country Boy." KPBS. January 26, 2021. https://www.kpbs.org/news/2015/mar/19/john-denver-country-boy/.

12. Khomami, Nadia. "Bruce Springsteen Says Years of Depression Left Him 'Crushed.'" *Guardian,* September 7, 2016, https://www.theguardian.com/music/2016/sep/07/bruce-springsteen-depression-crushed-born-to-run.

13. Gary Sinise Foundation. "Gary Sinise Biography." Accessed August 4, 2021. https://www.garysinisefoundation.org/founder/bio/.

14. Wong, Leon. "Sinise Receives Honor for Decades of Service." US Department of Defense. February 12, 2020. https://www.defense.gov/Explore/Features/story/Article/2081852/sinise-receives-honor-for-decades-of-service/.

15. Sanchez, Chelsey. "Demi Lovato Launches a Mental Health Fund for Those Struggling amid Coronavirus." *Harper's Bazaar,* April 22, 2020, https://www.harpersbazaar.com/celebrity/latest/a32236691/demi-lovato-launches-mental-health-fund-coronavirus/.

16. Clara Lionel Foundation. "$15 Million to Support Mental Health." June 18, 2020. https://claralionelfoundation.org/news/supporting-mental-health-services-during-covid-19/.

17. National Alliance on Mental Illness. "Mental Health by the Numbers." Accessed August 4, 2021. https://www.nami.org/mhstats.

18. Boris Lawrence Henson Foundation. "Home Page." Accessed August 4, 2021. https://borislhensonfoundation.org/.

5. Develop a Resilient Mindset

1. Cherry, Kendra. "What is Meditation." VeryWellMind. September 1, 2020. https://www.verywellmind.com/what-is-meditation-2795927.

6. Send Positive Vibes to Get Positive Results

1. Feloni, Richard. "9 Habits of Exceptional Leaders, According to the Classic Book 'How to Win Friends and Influence People.'" Insider. March 24, 2015. https://www.businessinsider.com/dale-carnegie-on-leadership-habits-2015-3.

8. University Life after Military Service

1. Sharon, Faye, and Joel Hooper. "Emotional Strength: A Response Type, Response Disposition and Organizing Principle for Emotion Experience." *New Ideas in Psychology* 50 (Aug 2018): 6-20. https://doi.org/10.1016/j.newideapsych.2018.02.002.
2. Yale University. "RULER Approach." Accessed July 7, 2021. https://www.rulerapproach.org/.

10. Using Music as Therapy

1. American Music Therapy Association. "Music Therapy and Military Populations." *A Status Report and Recommendations on Music Therapy Treatment, Programs, Research, and Practice Policy*, 2014. http://www.musictherapy.org/assets/1/7/MusicTherapyMilitaryPops_2014.pdf.
2. Raglio, Alfredo. "Music Therapy Interventions in Parkinson's Disease: The State-of-the-Art." *Frontiers in Neuroscience* 6, no. 185 (2015). https://doi.org/10.3389/fneur.2015.00185.

3. Houston, Elaine. "A Look at the Clinical Uses of Music Therapy." Positive Psychology. May 20, 2021. https://positivepsychology.com/music-therapy-clinical/.
4. University of Central Florida. "Your Brain on Music." *Pegasus,* accessed August 5, 2021, https://www.ucf.edu/pegasus/your-brain-on-music/.
5. Aggarwal-Schifellite, Manisha. "Frère Jacques, Are You Sleeping?" *Harvard Gazette,* October 19, 2020, https://news.harvard.edu/gazette/story/2020/10/research-shows-lullabies-in-any-language-relax-babies/.

11. Learn Something New Every Day

1. American Institute of Stress. "America's #1 Health Problem." Accessed August 5, 2021. https://www.stress.org/americas-1-health-problem.

12. Heal with Food, Sleep, and Exercise

1. Raypole, Crystal. "6 Ways to Boost Serotonin Without Medication." Healthline. April 22, 2019. https://www.healthline.com/health/how-to-increase-serotonin#diet.
2. Aubrey, Allison. "Food-Mood Connection: How You Eat Can Amp Up or Tamp Down Stress." NPR. July 14, 2014. https://www.npr.org/sections/thesalt/2014/07/14/329529110/food-mood-connection-how-you-eat-can-amp-up-or-tamp-down-stress.
3. Beccutia, Guglielmo, and Silvana Pannaina. "Sleep and Obesity." *Current Opinion in Clinical Nutrition and Metabolic Care* 14, no. 4 (2011): 402–412. https://doi.org/10.1097/MCO.0b013e3283479109.
4. "Sleep and Mental Health: Sleep Deprivation Can Affect Your Mental Health." Harvard Health Publishing. March 18, 2019. https://www.health.harvard.edu/newsletter_article/sleep-and-mental-health.
5. BelleVie International. "Sleep and Hormone Imbalance." Accessed July 8, 2021. https://bellevieinternational.com/sleep-hormone-imbalance/.

6. Olson, Eric. "Lack of sleep: Can It Make You Sick?" Expert Answers, Mayo Clinic. November 28, 2018. https://www.mayoclinic.org/diseases-conditions/insomnia/expert-answers/lack-of-sleep/faq-20057757.

7. "Benefits of Physical Activity." Centers for Disease Control and Prevention. Last reviewed April 5, 2021. https://www.cdc.gov/physicalactivity/basics/pa-health/index.htm.

My Special Gift to You!

1. Rizzi, Sofia. "The 30 Most Relaxing Songs Ever Have Been Revealed, According to Brits." Smooth Radio. Last updated September 2, 2019. https://www.smoothradio.com/news/music/most-relaxing-songs-list-poll/.

ABOUT THE AUTHOR

CSM Sa'eed Mustafa (formerly known as Tyrone Foster-King of Highland Falls, New York) is a post-9/11 era Army combat veteran. He joined the US Army in May of 1984 in Albany, New York. He served over thirty years in the military and retired from active duty on October 8, 2014, in front of family and friends at the United States Military Academy, West Point, New York.

He has already begun to explore his next literary project. Through strategic partnerships with Thorncroft Equestrian Center in Pennsylvania and Lazy J's Ranch in Massachusetts, CSM Mustafa will share his journey and learnings on the therapeutic power of horses for veterans with PTSD.

For more updates:
https://csmsaeedmustafa.com/

facebook.com/OfficialSaeedMustafa

twitter.com/CSM_Mustafa

instagram.com/csm_mustafa

linkedin.com/in/csm-saeed-mustafa-7308ab43

Made in the USA
Monee, IL
02 May 2022

f1b12ed9-9cc2-4c2f-a7b3-d3a5ea6dddc2R01